ASSESSMENT

Vocabulary Workshop Tests
Fourth Course

- Standardized Test Formats for
    - Analogies
    - Sentence Completions
    - Reading Passages
- Lesson Tests

HOLT, RINEHART AND WINSTON

A Harcourt Classroom Education Company

Austin • New York • Orlando • Atlanta • San Francisco • Boston • Dallas • Toronto • London

EDITORIAL
Director
Mescal Evler
Manager of Editorial Operations
Bill Wahlgren
Executive Editor
Emily G. Shenk
Project Editor
Cheryl L. Christian
Writing and Editing: Janis D. Russell
Editorial Assistant: Kim Soriano
Copyediting: Michael Neibergall, *Copyediting Manager;* Mary Malone, *Senior Copyeditor;* Joel Bourgeois, Elizabeth Dickson, Gabrielle Field, Jane Kominek, Millicent Ondras, Theresa Reding, Kathleen Scheiner, Laurie Schlesinger, *Copyeditors*
Project Administration: Marie Price, *Managing Editor;* Lori De La Garza, *Editorial Operations Coordinator;* Thomas Browne, Heather Cheyne, Diane Hardin, Mark Holland, Marcus Johnson, Jill O'Neal, Joyce Rector, Janet Riley, Kelly Tankersley, *Project Administration;* Gail Coupland, Ruth Hooker, Margaret Sanchez, *Word Processing*
Editorial Permissions: Janet Harrington, *Permissions Editor*

ART, DESIGN AND PHOTO
Graphic Services
Kristen Darby, *Manager*
Image Acquisitions: Joe London, *Director;* Tim Taylor, *Photo Research Supervisor;* Rick Benavides, *Assistant Photo Researcher;* Elaine Tate, *Supervisor;* Erin Cone, *Art Buyer*
Cover Design
Sunday Patterson

PRODUCTION
Belinda Barbosa Lopez, *Senior Production Coordinator;* Simira Davis, *Supervisor;* Nancy Hargis, *Media Production Supervisor;* Joan Lindsay, *Production Coordinator;* Beth Prevelige, *Prepress Manager*

ELECTRONIC PUBLISHING
Carol Martin, *Senior Electronic Publishing Manager;* Robert Franklin, *Electronic Publishing Manager;* Indira Konanur, *Project Coordinator;* JoAnn Brown, Richard Chavez, Jim Gaile, Heather Jernt, Lana Kaupp, Christopher Lucas, Robin McKinney, Nanda Patel, *EP staff;* Emilie Keturakis, Katelijne Lefevere, Sally Williams, *Quality Control Coordinators*

MANUFACTURING
Michael Roche, *Supervisor of Inventory and Manufacturing*

Copyright © by Holt, Rinehart and Winston

All rights reserved. No part of this publication may be reproduced or transmitted in any form or by any means, electronic or mechanical, including photocopy, recording, or any information storage and retrieval system, without permission in writing from the publisher.

Teachers using ELEMENTS OF LANGUAGE may photocopy blackline masters in complete pages in sufficient quantities for classroom use only and not for resale.

Printed in the United States of America

ISBN 0-03-056302-X

4 5 6 7 8   023   09 08 07 06 05

Contents

Note to the Teacher iv

Formative Assessment 1

> Each test corresponds to a lesson in
> Making New Words Your Own
>   Lessons 1–30

Test 1 3
Test 2 4
Test 3 5
Test 4 6
Test 5 7
Test 6 8
Test 7 9
Test 8 10
Test 9 11
Test 10 12
Test 11 13
Test 12 14
Test 13 15
Test 14 16
Test 15 17
Test 16 18
Test 17 19
Test 18 20
Test 19 21
Test 20 22
Test 21 23
Test 22 24
Test 23 25
Test 24 26
Test 25 27
Test 26 28
Test 27 29
Test 28 30
Test 29 31
Test 30 32

Summative Assessment 33

Test 1   CONTEXT: Expression 35

> This test covers the first 100 words as they
> are presented in—
> • Making New Words Your Own
>   Lessons 1–10
> • Connecting New Words and Patterns
>   Lessons 1–5
> • Reading New Words in Context
>   Lessons 1–5

    PART A • Critical Reading 35
    PART B • Sentence Completion 39
    PART C • Analogies 44

Test 2   CONTEXT: Civilization 47

> This test covers the second 100 words as
> they are presented in—
> • Making New Words Your Own
>   Lessons 11–20
> • Connecting New Words and Patterns
>   Lessons 6–10
> • Reading New Words in Context
>   Lessons 6–10

    PART A • Critical Reading 47
    PART B • Sentence Completion 51
    PART C • Analogies 56

Test 3   CONTEXT: The Environment 59

> This test covers the third 100 words as they
> are presented in—
> • Making New Words Your Own
>   Lessons 21–30
> • Connecting New Words and Patterns
>   Lessons 11–15
> • Reading New Words in Context
>   Lessons 11–15

    PART A • Critical Reading 59
    PART B • Sentence Completion 63
    PART C • Analogies 68

NOTE TO THE TEACHER

This booklet contains one section of formative assessment and one section of summative assessment. The formative assessment section includes one test for each of the thirty lessons included in the Making New Words Your Own phase of *Vocabulary Workshop*.

The summative assessment section consists of three tests. Each summative test corresponds to ten of the lessons in Making New Words Your Own, five of the lessons in Connecting New Words and Patterns, and five of the lessons in Reading New Words in Context.

The answers for each test are included in a separate answer key booklet. The point scoring for each test follows the directions for each part of that test. The total score for each test is 100 points.

FORMATIVE ASSESSMENT

Tests 1–30

Name _____ Date _____ Class _____

USING NEW WORDS ON TESTS

Test 1

Directions. In the space provided, write the letter of the word or phrase closest in meaning to the boldface word. *(10 points each)*

____ 1. the defendant's **acquittal**
  (A) line of defense
  (B) being set free
  (C) guilty verdict
  (D) trial lawyer
  (E) guilty behavior

____ 2. to **assert** one's rights
  (A) declare firmly
  (B) deny or give up
  (C) plead for
  (D) fail to appreciate
  (E) forget about

____ 3. to **condescend** to someone
  (A) look
  (B) speak
  (C) stoop
  (D) shout
  (E) whisper

____ 4. a **contemptuous** act
  (A) scornful
  (B) humble
  (C) dramatic
  (D) friendly
  (E) criminal

____ 5. friends of the **elite**
  (A) poor people
  (B) recent immigrants
  (C) powerful group
  (D) concerned citizens
  (E) art scholars

____ 6. to **evolve** a plan
  (A) follow closely
  (B) set forth
  (C) attempt to cancel
  (D) develop gradually
  (E) criticize severely

____ 7. to show **fortitude**
  (A) fairness
  (B) endurance
  (C) generosity
  (D) concern
  (E) equality

____ 8. **inarticulate** answers
  (A) clever
  (B) thoughtful
  (C) polite
  (D) angry
  (E) unclear

____ 9. to listen to your **mentor**
  (A) symphony
  (B) teammate
  (C) advisor
  (D) prediction
  (E) idea

____ 10. to have **notoriety**
  (A) ill fame
  (B) great worth
  (C) immense wealth
  (D) vast sympathy
  (E) a chance

Name _____ Date _____ Class _____

USING NEW WORDS ON TESTS

Test 2

Directions. In the space provided, write the letter of the word or phrase closest in meaning to the boldface word. *(10 points each)*

____ 1. make the **analogy**
- (A) picture
- (B) conclusion
- (C) effort
- (D) comparison
- (E) opportunity

____ 2. relics of **antiquity**
- (A) Revolutionary times
- (B) ancient times
- (C) the city of Atlantis
- (D) the good old days
- (E) foreign ancestors

____ 3. to satisfy the **electorate**
- (A) voters
- (B) legislature
- (C) judiciary
- (D) legislators
- (E) president

____ 4. **ethical** conduct
- (A) questionable
- (B) characteristic
- (C) personal
- (D) moral
- (E) rude

____ 5. a brief **excerpt**
- (A) opening statement
- (B) children's book
- (C) selected passage
- (D) comic play
- (E) lyric poem

____ 6. to teach a **heresy**
- (A) scientific theory
- (B) dialect of a language
- (C) skill used in technology
- (D) idea that opposes standard beliefs
- (E) method for people to improve themselves

____ 7. **paternal** feelings
- (A) brotherly
- (B) motherly
- (C) angry
- (D) familiar
- (E) fatherly

____ 8. pity for a **pauper**
- (A) recently sentenced criminal
- (B) terminally ill person
- (C) very poor person
- (D) seriously injured person
- (E) very wealthy person

____ 9. her **posthumous** award
- (A) hard-earned
- (B) after-death
- (C) foreign
- (D) historical
- (E) current

____ 10. **prophetic** powers
- (A) physical
- (B) fearsome
- (C) magical
- (D) unlawful
- (E) predictive

4 FORMATIVE ASSESSMENT

Using New Words on Tests

Test 3

Directions. In the space provided, write the letter of the word or phrase closest in meaning to the boldface word. *(10 points each)*

____ 1. **amiable** people
(A) elderly
(B) pleasant
(C) ugly
(D) purposeful
(E) harmful

____ 2. a saltwater **bayou**
(A) game fish
(B) marshy inlet
(C) sailing craft
(D) artificial lake
(E) dry gully

____ 3. to **grimace** in pain
(A) seek aid
(B) scream out
(C) make a face
(D) remain quiet
(E) move about

____ 4. **indomitable** courage
(A) little
(B) faltering
(C) rash
(D) unyielding
(E) insufficient

____ 5. **malleable** personalities
(A) kind
(B) unchangeable
(C) lovable
(D) rugged
(E) adaptive

____ 6. the **melodramatic** story
(A) unexciting
(B) complex
(C) prizewinning
(D) sentimental
(E) interesting

____ 7. to **succumb** to temptation
(A) yield
(B) resist
(C) lead
(D) ignore
(E) follow

____ 8. **vibrant** streets
(A) newly paved
(B) throbbing with activity
(C) mysteriously empty
(D) poorly lighted
(E) crowded with children

____ 9. a man's **visage**
(A) temperament
(B) foot
(C) size
(D) emotions
(E) face

____ 10. a **whimsical** story
(A) fanciful
(B) moving
(C) serious
(D) dull
(E) comical

Name _____ Date _____ Class _____

USING NEW WORDS ON TESTS

Test 4

Directions. In the space provided, write the letter of the word or phrase closest in meaning to the boldface word. *(10 points each)*

____ 1. an **apprehensive** person
   (A) accused
   (B) anxious
   (C) uncaring
   (D) unusual
   (E) sleepy

____ 2. his **callous** answer
   (A) sensitive
   (B) funny
   (C) loud
   (D) unfeeling
   (E) creative

____ 3. a **commendable** action
   (A) quick
   (B) thoughtful
   (C) praiseworthy
   (D) delayed
   (E) forced

____ 4. **indignant** responses
   (A) angry
   (B) humble
   (C) apologetic
   (D) unintelligent
   (E) quiet

____ 5. an **ineffectual** leader
   (A) uncaring
   (B) inspiring
   (C) involved
   (D) unbeatable
   (E) inadequate

____ 6. **judicious** moves
   (A) wise
   (B) official
   (C) legal
   (D) political
   (E) familiar

____ 7. a famous **mystic**
   (A) talented teacher
   (B) undercover detective
   (C) religious seeker
   (D) laboratory scientist
   (E) Shakespearean actor

____ 8. to **paraphrase** a poem
   (A) restate
   (B) recite
   (C) create
   (D) select
   (E) memorize

____ 9. the **personification** of evil
   (A) danger
   (B) fear
   (C) recognition
   (D) representation
   (E) director

____ 10. a **verbatim** quote
   (A) famous
   (B) word-for-word
   (C) long and dreary
   (D) repeated incorrectly
   (E) time-honored

Using New Words on Tests

Test 5

Directions. In the space provided, write the letter of the word or phrase closest in meaning to the boldface word. *(10 points each)*

____ 1. two firms that **affiliate**
   (A) agree
   (B) associate
   (C) compete
   (D) separate
   (E) provide

____ 2. an **exalted** style of writing
   (A) excited
   (B) unorganized
   (C) elevated
   (D) studious
   (E) literary

____ 3. to **encumber** oneself
   (A) burden
   (B) prepare
   (C) educate
   (D) calm
   (E) understand

____ 4. questions that **invariably** challenge
   (A) occasionally
   (B) frequently
   (C) sometimes
   (D) eventually
   (E) always

____ 5. a **plausible** explanation
   (A) ridiculous
   (B) clear
   (C) reasonable
   (D) wise
   (E) false

____ 6. a **pompous** person
   (A) self-important
   (B) stout
   (C) timid
   (D) enthusiastic
   (E) well-known

____ 7. a **portly** gentleman
   (A) thin
   (B) undignified
   (C) stout
   (D) influential
   (E) timid

____ 8. to be in **proximity**
   (A) fear
   (B) nearness
   (C) trouble
   (D) expectation
   (E) favor

____ 9. to **rejuvenate** the body
   (A) care for
   (B) exercise regularly
   (C) risk injury to
   (D) make young
   (E) wear out

____ 10. the **unprecedented** story
   (A) typical
   (B) long
   (C) unique
   (D) funny
   (E) recited

Name _____ Date _____ Class _____

USING NEW WORDS ON TESTS

Test 6

Directions. In the space provided, write the letter of the word or phrase closest in meaning to the boldface word. *(10 points each)*

_____ 1. **atrocious** spelling
 (A) simple
 (B) complicated
 (C) correct
 (D) bad
 (E) tricky

_____ 2. to feel **compassion**
 (A) anger
 (B) fear
 (C) sympathy
 (D) dislike
 (E) nothing

_____ 3. to have **composure** on stage
 (A) calmness
 (B) talent
 (C) fright
 (D) direction
 (E) lights

_____ 4. buildings that **deteriorate**
 (A) improve
 (B) have great height
 (C) increase
 (D) worsen
 (E) are abandoned

_____ 5. to **discern** his motives
 (A) identify
 (B) honor
 (C) ignore
 (D) overlook
 (E) criticize

_____ 6. **insipid** meals
 (A) tasty
 (B) family
 (C) late
 (D) big
 (E) flavorless

_____ 7. to sing a **lament**
 (A) love song
 (B) poetic expression of grief
 (C) advertisement jingle
 (D) French roundelay
 (E) popular song

_____ 8. to **loathe** something
 (A) admire
 (B) envy
 (C) expect
 (D) detest
 (E) uphold

_____ 9. **painstaking** tasks
 (A) easy
 (B) meticulous
 (C) painful
 (D) thankless
 (E) pointless

_____ 10. to **repress** your anger
 (A) restrain
 (B) release
 (C) avoid
 (D) incite
 (E) scream

Using New Words on Tests

Test 7

Directions. In the space provided, write the letter of the word or phrase closest in meaning to the boldface word. *(10 points each)*

_____ 1. **aesthetic** judgment
   (A) insensitive
   (B) good
   (C) unqualified
   (D) clear
   (E) artistic

_____ 2. to have **charisma**
   (A) leadership quality
   (B) fear of failure
   (C) proof of purchase
   (D) common sense
   (E) strong opinions

_____ 3. an old **cliché**
   (A) bit of advice
   (B) trite expression
   (C) silly idea
   (D) negative belief
   (E) persistent problem

_____ 4. to **conceive** an idea
   (A) criticize
   (B) develop
   (C) study
   (D) forget
   (E) offer

_____ 5. to speak **emphatically**
   (A) quietly
   (B) calmly
   (C) angrily
   (D) forcefully
   (E) truthfully

_____ 6. **martial** law
   (A) military
   (B) unfair
   (C) strict
   (D) easy
   (E) state

_____ 7. presented with a **paradox**
   (A) welcome gift
   (B) commencement speech
   (C) alternate solution
   (D) seeming contradiction
   (E) rare opportunity

_____ 8. the **prolific** author
   (A) poor
   (B) productive
   (C) unknown
   (D) famous
   (E) wealthy

_____ 9. a happy **recipient**
   (A) scholar
   (B) worker
   (C) recruit
   (D) receiver
   (E) friend

_____ 10. her **wan** face
   (A) joyful
   (B) angry
   (C) pale
   (D) red
   (E) smiling

Name _____ Date _____ Class _____

USING NEW WORDS ON TESTS

Test 8

Directions. In the space provided, write the letter of the word or phrase closest in meaning to the boldface word. *(10 points each)*

_____ 1. an **aura** of brightness
   (A) rainbow
   (B) moment
   (C) cover
   (D) awareness
   (E) glow

_____ 2. tends to **fabricate**
   (A) invent
   (B) copy
   (C) repeat
   (D) overestimate
   (E) promise

_____ 3. the **impediment** on the path
   (A) scenery
   (B) surface
   (C) danger
   (D) obstruction
   (E) crossing

_____ 4. a **mediocre** movie
   (A) average
   (B) excellent
   (C) popular
   (D) silent
   (E) boring

_____ 5. the **opportune** moment
   (A) unexpected
   (B) brief
   (C) suitable
   (D) pleasurable
   (E) final

_____ 6. to have **qualms** about moving
   (A) excitement
   (B) misgivings
   (C) anxiety
   (D) choices
   (E) thoughts

_____ 7. **reactionary** positions
   (A) unclearly stated
   (B) resisting new ideas
   (C) remain silent about
   (D) rejecting old ideas
   (E) carefully worded

_____ 8. to have great **stamina**
   (A) suffering
   (B) wealth
   (C) interest
   (D) rewards
   (E) endurance

_____ 9. **zealous** people
   (A) indifferent
   (B) smart
   (C) eager
   (D) angry
   (E) pleasant

_____ 10. the gentle **zephyr**
   (A) hand
   (B) echo
   (C) lamb
   (D) breeze
   (E) rain

Using New Words on Tests

Test 9

Directions. In the space provided, write the letter of the word or phrase closest in meaning to the boldface word. *(10 points each)*

____ 1. repeat the **axiom**
 (A) self-evident truth
 (B) nonsense
 (C) gossip
 (D) well-known poem
 (E) speech

____ 2. **compatible** neighbors
 (A) disagreeable
 (B) distant
 (C) harmonious
 (D) nearby
 (E) unknown

____ 3. an act of **compliance**
 (A) refusal
 (B) opposition
 (C) yielding
 (D) kindness
 (E) forgiveness

____ 4. **inanimate** objects
 (A) new
 (B) cherished
 (C) pretty
 (D) small
 (E) lifeless

____ 5. **indestructible** plastic
 (A) unbeatable
 (B) unbreakable
 (C) incredible
 (D) inflammable
 (E) bendable

____ 6. **innate** traits
 (A) inborn
 (B) good
 (C) undesirable
 (D) learned
 (E) uncharacteristic

____ 7. a **mutable** temperament
 (A) steady
 (B) silent
 (C) sad
 (D) changeable
 (E) courageous

____ 8. to have sharp **perceptions**
 (A) expectations
 (B) differences
 (C) methods
 (D) impressions
 (E) schemes

____ 9. a **prevalent** disease
 (A) curable
 (B) rare
 (C) deadly
 (D) widespread
 (E) crippling

____ 10. his only **recourse**
 (A) money
 (B) help
 (C) knowledge
 (D) excuse
 (E) purpose

Name _____ Date _____ Class _____

USING NEW WORDS ON TESTS

Test 10

Directions. In the space provided, write the letter of the word or phrase closest in meaning to the boldface word. *(10 points each)*

____ 1. to **encompass** an idea
  (A) express
  (B) explore
  (C) study
  (D) include
  (E) support

____ 2. her **implacable** enemy
  (A) shifty
  (B) angry
  (C) former
  (D) weak
  (E) relentless

____ 3. the **incentive** to study
  (A) agreement
  (B) unwillingness
  (C) need
  (D) assignment
  (E) motivation

____ 4. a well-known **militant**
  (A) sailor
  (B) advisor
  (C) leader
  (D) activist
  (E) governor

____ 5. his **pivotal** decision
  (A) crucial
  (B) final
  (C) unfortunate
  (D) amazing
  (E) thoughtful

____ 6. to **postulate** an idea
  (A) postpone
  (B) assume
  (C) review
  (D) anticipate
  (E) withdraw

____ 7. receive **retribution**
  (A) punishment
  (B) pardon
  (C) permission
  (D) scorn
  (E) advice

____ 8. **stringent** laws
  (A) relaxed
  (B) out-of-date
  (C) strict
  (D) newly passed
  (E) short-lived

____ 9. to **transcend** something
  (A) do without
  (B) criticize sharply
  (C) give away
  (D) rise above
  (E) enjoy immensely

____ 10. a **transitory** feeling
  (A) lasting
  (B) temporary
  (C) strong
  (D) joyous
  (E) unpleasant

Using New Words on Tests

Test 11

Directions. In the space provided, write the letter of the word or phrase closest in meaning to the boldface word. *(10 points each)*

_____ 1. to have **autonomy**
   (A) independence
   (B) hope
   (C) needs
   (D) transportation
   (E) dependency

_____ 2. to **besiege** a fort
   (A) guard against attack
   (B) surround in order to capture
   (C) begin building
   (D) reinforce the walls of
   (E) arrive at

_____ 3. great **devastation**
   (A) destruction
   (B) construction
   (C) expanse
   (D) ability
   (E) opportunity

_____ 4. **inclement** weather
   (A) pleasant
   (B) hot
   (C) uncertain
   (D) stormy
   (E) humid

_____ 5. the **latitude** to act
   (A) reluctance
   (B) freedom
   (C) readiness
   (D) plan
   (E) desire

_____ 6. a habit of **perseverance**
   (A) steadfastness
   (B) quitting
   (C) pretending
   (D) forgetting
   (E) following

_____ 7. **precarious** positions
   (A) safe
   (B) established
   (C) dangerous
   (D) important
   (E) unknown

_____ 8. **vulnerable** environments
   (A) protected
   (B) hostile
   (C) unprotected
   (D) safe
   (E) forested

_____ 9. brilliance that will **wane**
   (A) increase
   (B) illuminate
   (C) decrease
   (D) blind
   (E) protect

_____ 10. to **wreak** havoc
   (A) fear
   (B) stop
   (C) explore
   (D) prevent
   (E) inflict

Name _____ Date _____ Class _____

USING NEW WORDS ON TESTS

Test 12

Directions. In the space provided, write the letter of the word or phrase closest in meaning to the boldface word. *(10 points each)*

___ 1. to **appease** someone
   (A) dislike
   (B) delay
   (C) pacify
   (D) anger
   (E) help

___ 2. **archaic** expressions
   (A) strong
   (B) beautiful
   (C) encouraging
   (D) outdated
   (E) famous

___ 3. **balmy** weather
   (A) cold
   (B) rainy
   (C) hot
   (D) mild
   (E) stormy

___ 4. to **beguile** someone
   (A) deceive
   (B) accompany
   (C) like
   (D) hate
   (E) support

___ 5. to **commence** a ceremony
   (A) begin
   (B) take part in
   (C) observe
   (D) walk out of
   (E) speak in

___ 6. engaged in **espionage**
   (A) exercise
   (B) housekeeping
   (C) studying
   (D) teaching
   (E) spying

___ 7. a reasonable **facsimile**
   (A) answer
   (B) reproduction
   (C) excuse
   (D) deadline
   (E) promise

___ 8. an **invincible** rival
   (A) injured
   (B) unseen
   (C) unconquerable
   (D) absent
   (E) frightening

___ 9. created a **pretext**
   (A) similar pattern
   (B) different problem
   (C) careful plan
   (D) written schedule
   (E) false reason

___ 10. **vigilant** people
   (A) proud
   (B) watchful
   (C) quiet
   (D) angry
   (E) victorious

14 FORMATIVE ASSESSMENT

USING NEW WORDS ON TESTS

Test 13

Directions. In the space provided, write the letter of the word or phrase closest in meaning to the boldface word. *(10 points each)*

_____ 1. a **coffer** of gold
  (A) cross
  (B) chunk
  (C) chest
  (D) gift
  (E) necklace

_____ 2. a large **edifice**
  (A) estate
  (B) building
  (C) plantation
  (D) tree
  (E) program

_____ 3. **hieroglyphic** writing
  (A) sophisticated
  (B) poetic
  (C) ceremonial
  (D) picture
  (E) creative

_____ 4. **inaccessible** places
  (A) pleasant and inviting
  (B) dark and scary
  (C) out-of-doors
  (D) quiet and peaceful
  (E) out-of-the-way

_____ 5. a great **innovation**
  (A) relaxed outing
  (B) charitable contribution
  (C) something new
  (D) meeting of minds
  (E) annual celebration

_____ 6. at this **juncture**
  (A) panel discussion
  (B) point in time
  (C) way station
  (D) full stop
  (E) lunch appointment

_____ 7. to pay the **retainer**
  (A) advance payment
  (B) final fee
  (C) overdue bill
  (D) inflated price
  (E) bank fee

_____ 8. a nearby **rivulet**
  (A) swift river
  (B) quiet park
  (C) small stream
  (D) wide river
  (E) large lake

_____ 9. to **subsidize** something
  (A) bring back to a former condition
  (B) support with a grant of money
  (C) subscribe to
  (D) seek financial contributions for
  (E) apply for a patent

_____ 10. the **tawny** lion
  (A) tired
  (B) ferocious
  (C) angry
  (D) tan
  (E) large

Using New Words on Tests

Test 14

Directions. In the space provided, write the letter of the word or phrase closest in meaning to the boldface word. *(10 points each)*

____ 1. the mountain's **apex**
  (A) steep slope
  (B) low timberline
  (C) fertile terrain
  (D) highest point
  (E) spectacular view

____ 2. **bourgeois** values
  (A) lower-class
  (B) middle-class
  (C) upper-class
  (D) foreign
  (E) common

____ 3. to own a **canine**
  (A) cat
  (B) bird
  (C) dog
  (D) horse
  (E) rabbit

____ 4. **defunct** ideas
  (A) popular
  (B) proven
  (C) funny
  (D) outdated
  (E) foolish

____ 5. the **influx** of students
  (A) flowing in
  (B) small number
  (C) constant turnover
  (D) flowing out
  (E) coming together

____ 6. **meager** supplies
  (A) satisfactory
  (B) scanty
  (C) plentiful
  (D) useful
  (E) ideal

____ 7. to **obliterate** a forest
  (A) observe closely
  (B) write about
  (C) walk through
  (D) explore thoroughly
  (E) wipe out

____ 8. wood that began to **ossify**
  (A) harden
  (B) burn quickly
  (C) dry out
  (D) rot away
  (E) dampen

____ 9. to **perceive** a clue
  (A) detect
  (B) plant
  (C) hint about
  (D) cover up
  (E) follow

____ 10. to **ravage** the town
  (A) build
  (B) alarm
  (C) destroy
  (D) save
  (E) improve

Using New Words on Tests

Test 15

Directions. In the space provided, write the letter of the word or phrase closest in meaning to the boldface word. *(10 points each)*

____ 1. a sumptuous **buffet**
(A) late-night snack
(B) expensive dessert
(C) self-served meal
(D) formal dinner
(E) French soup

____ 2. **delectable** food
(A) delicatessen
(B) nutritious
(C) exotic
(D) delicious
(E) foreign

____ 3. events that **ensue**
(A) follow
(B) extend over
(C) last a long time
(D) change
(E) slow down

____ 4. an **expedient** method
(A) unsuitable
(B) old
(C) understood
(D) uncommon
(E) advantageous

____ 5. to **facilitate** something
(A) hinder
(B) ignore
(C) discuss
(D) aid
(E) report

____ 6. tasted the **hors d'oeuvre**
(A) hot beverage
(B) dessert
(C) appetizer
(D) light meal
(E) breakfast

____ 7. a **lapse** in manners
(A) needed lesson
(B) temporary slip
(C) showy display
(D) total unconcern
(E) vast improvement

____ 8. **palatable** food
(A) tasty
(B) spoiled
(C) insufficient
(D) abundant
(E) healthy

____ 9. the wild **steppe**
(A) forest
(B) mountains
(C) desert
(D) ocean
(E) plain

____ 10. the **succulent** roast
(A) edible
(B) small
(C) spicy
(D) juicy
(E) fatty

USING NEW WORDS ON TESTS

Test 16

Directions. In the space provided, write the letter of the word or phrase closest in meaning to the boldface word. *(10 points each)*

____ 1. **aptitude** for math
   (A) test
   (B) study
   (C) ability
   (D) problems
   (E) answers

____ 2. **astute** observations
   (A) obvious
   (B) shrewd
   (C) humane
   (D) scientific
   (E) random

____ 3. **conducive** to victory
   (A) unhelpful
   (B) striving
   (C) fearless
   (D) helpful
   (E) critical

____ 4. **erratic** behavior
   (A) regular
   (B) perfect
   (C) steady
   (D) irregular
   (E) serious

____ 5. design a **mosque**
   (A) resort hotel
   (B) house of worship
   (C) suspension bridge
   (D) unique disguise
   (E) underground tunnel

____ 6. **pastoral** settings
   (A) interior
   (B) rural
   (C) urban
   (D) religious
   (E) exterior

____ 7. measured in **quantitative** ways
   (A) according to numerical amount
   (B) according to human emotions
   (C) according to excellence
   (D) according to rank
   (E) according to intelligence

____ 8. not allowed to **recur**
   (A) get out
   (B) finish early
   (C) happen again
   (D) take place
   (E) get in

____ 9. a **requisite** for graduation
   (A) gown
   (B) diploma
   (C) requirement
   (D) speech
   (E) rehearsal

____ 10. the **zenith** of a career
   (A) high point
   (B) low point
   (C) promising beginning
   (D) critical decision
   (E) high expectation

Using New Words on Tests

Test 17

Directions. In the space provided, write the letter of the word or phrase closest in meaning to the boldface word. *(10 points each)*

___ 1. **annihilate** the enemy
   (A) forgive
   (B) attack
   (C) harm
   (D) destroy
   (E) support

___ 2. a major **concession**
   (A) decision on tax
   (B) act of yielding
   (C) internal policy
   (D) federal law
   (E) complete understanding

___ 3. to **decimate** the troops
   (A) flee from
   (B) count on completely
   (C) surrender to
   (D) destroy a large part of
   (E) provide for

___ 4. a childish **diversion**
   (A) pastime
   (B) feeling
   (C) idea
   (D) act
   (E) smile

___ 5. to **evade** questions
   (A) ask
   (B) discuss
   (C) avoid
   (D) answer
   (E) discover

___ 6. **flagrant** behavior
   (A) unusual
   (B) ordinary
   (C) funny
   (D) rude
   (E) outrageous

___ 7. unforgivable **insolence**
   (A) misbehavior
   (B) humiliation
   (C) disrespect
   (D) laziness
   (E) thoughts

___ 8. everything in **moderation**
   (A) no extremes
   (B) total confusion
   (C) large amounts
   (D) total agreement
   (E) order of importance

___ 9. **prone** to jealousy
   (A) unyielding
   (B) resistant
   (C) inclined
   (D) opposed
   (E) indebted

___ 10. to **purge** from government
   (A) gain approval
   (B) take orders
   (C) rid
   (D) receive praise
   (E) rule

Using New Words on Tests

Test 18

Directions. In the space provided, write the letter of the word or phrase closest in meaning to the boldface word. *(10 points each)*

____ 1. to show **clemency**
   (A) promise
   (B) mercy
   (C) weakness
   (D) fierceness
   (E) emotions

____ 2. to **dissent** from the group
   (A) resign
   (B) seek support
   (C) differ
   (D) be forced
   (E) rotate

____ 3. a lack of **inhibition**
   (A) encouragement
   (B) ability
   (C) interest
   (D) moisture
   (E) restraint

____ 4. the **mandatory** penalty
   (A) harsh
   (B) light
   (C) optional
   (D) required
   (E) ideal

____ 5. a quaint **mannerism**
   (A) philosophy
   (B) habit
   (C) building
   (D) etiquette
   (E) personality

____ 6. **meticulous** handwork
   (A) sloppy
   (B) difficult
   (C) repetitive
   (D) mindless
   (E) precise

____ 7. a meeting of **pacifists**
   (A) believers in desertion
   (B) believers in negotiation
   (C) believers in nonviolence
   (D) believers in democracy
   (E) believers in kindness

____ 8. accepted **protocol**
   (A) diplomatic etiquette
   (B) proper behavior
   (C) standard of excellence
   (D) scientific method
   (E) international agreement

____ 9. complete **submission**
   (A) anger
   (B) fear
   (C) aggression
   (D) obedience
   (E) happiness

____ 10. an angry **ultimatum**
   (A) commander in chief
   (B) crowd of people
   (C) final demand
   (D) sudden attack
   (E) official protest

Name _____ Date _____ Class _____

USING NEW WORDS ON TESTS

Test 19

Directions. In the space provided, write the letter of the word or phrase closest in meaning to the boldface word. *(10 points each)*

____ 1. animals that **abound**
   (A) jump high
   (B) eat meat
   (C) run away
   (D) are rare
   (E) are plentiful

____ 2. to behave **admirably**
   (A) excellently
   (B) jealously
   (C) badly
   (D) cruelly
   (E) emotionally

____ 3. to sign the **affidavit**
   (A) written statement
   (B) blank check
   (C) speeding ticket
   (D) job application
   (E) proposed law

____ 4. to grant **amnesty**
   (A) money
   (B) ideas
   (C) pardon
   (D) forgetfulness
   (E) supplies

____ 5. a **bias** against comic books
   (A) argument
   (B) boycott
   (C) campaign
   (D) policy
   (E) prejudice

____ 6. to **censure** someone
   (A) praise
   (B) argue with
   (C) criticize
   (D) agree with
   (E) forgive

____ 7. a **diminutive** hand
   (A) smooth
   (B) reddened
   (C) tiny
   (D) rough
   (E) dry

____ 8. **inalienable** rights
   (A) not to be taken away
   (B) carefully explained
   (C) not to be imposed
   (D) permanently suspended
   (E) not to be granted

____ 9. the **rift** in the ice
   (A) intense cold
   (B) split
   (C) air bubble
   (D) change of color
   (E) stripe

____ 10. a **timorous** dog
   (A) hungry
   (B) purebred
   (C) playful
   (D) cowardly
   (E) huge

USING NEW WORDS ON TESTS

USING NEW WORDS ON TESTS

Test 20

Directions. In the space provided, write the letter of the word or phrase closest in meaning to the boldface word. *(10 points each)*

____ 1. a scene of **bedlam**
 (A) beauty
 (B) confusion
 (C) restfulness
 (D) sorrow
 (E) creation

____ 2. **colloquial** expressions
 (A) happy
 (B) formal
 (C) sad
 (D) informal
 (E) unusual

____ 3. to **consolidate** debts
 (A) pay
 (B) release
 (C) list
 (D) forgive
 (E) combine

____ 4. represented the **constituents**
 (A) offenders
 (B) voters
 (C) amateurs
 (D) petitioners
 (E) executives

____ 5. to **curtail** our visit
 (A) arrange
 (B) shorten
 (C) lengthen
 (D) continue
 (E) enjoy

____ 6. **destitute** people
 (A) educated
 (B) elegant
 (C) imprisoned
 (D) penniless
 (E) powerful

____ 7. to **emancipate** the serfs
 (A) free
 (B) mistreat
 (C) study
 (D) imprison
 (E) support

____ 8. the **exultant** winner
 (A) jubilant
 (B) expected
 (C) unexpected
 (D) tired
 (E) challenged

____ 9. **ornate** costumes
 (A) pretty
 (B) unusual
 (C) elaborate
 (D) simple
 (E) heavy

____ 10. the **prelude** to disaster
 (A) road
 (B) witness
 (C) inclination
 (D) incentive
 (E) introduction

Using New Words on Tests

Test 21

Directions. In the space provided, write the letter of the word or phrase closest in meaning to the boldface word. *(10 points each)*

____ 1. to **bestride** a horse
   (A) saddle
   (B) walk
   (C) groom
   (D) straddle
   (E) own

____ 2. open a **casement**
   (A) chest
   (B) door
   (C) desktop
   (D) window
   (E) box

____ 3. an actor's **debut**
   (A) first performance
   (B) rise to fame
   (C) end of career
   (D) formal training
   (E) dress rehearsal

____ 4. watch a **documentary**
   (A) class play
   (B) factual program
   (C) holiday parade
   (D) lengthy program
   (E) legal program

____ 5. prices that **fluctuate**
   (A) fall
   (B) waver
   (C) stabilize
   (D) rise
   (E) please

____ 6. to feel **melancholy**
   (A) silky
   (B) outraged
   (C) nervous
   (D) lazy
   (E) depressed

____ 7. to grant a **reprieve**
   (A) request
   (B) favor
   (C) postponement
   (D) interruption
   (E) position

____ 8. to listen to the **requiem**
   (A) inspiring sermon
   (B) religious play
   (C) foolish suggestion
   (D) music to honor the dead
   (E) lecture for new students

____ 9. **theoretical** answers
   (A) correct
   (B) inaccurate
   (C) unproven
   (D) wordy
   (E) sharp

____ 10. his **vehement** argument
   (A) logical
   (B) sound
   (C) mild
   (D) intense
   (E) poisonous

USING NEW WORDS ON TESTS

Test 22

Directions. In the space provided, write the letter of the word or phrase closest in meaning to the boldface word. *(10 points each)*

____ 1. the **clangor** in the factory
 (A) work force
 (B) machinery
 (C) assembly line
 (D) loud sound
 (E) production

____ 2. to **enjoin** payment
 (A) refuse
 (B) command
 (C) postpone
 (D) offer
 (E) plan

____ 3. to **gloat** smugly
 (A) eat a large meal
 (B) take greedy pleasure
 (C) mock someone
 (D) argue against
 (E) refuse to attend

____ 4. to **indict** a suspect
 (A) officially arrest
 (B) follow
 (C) release
 (D) formally accuse
 (E) believe

____ 5. to leave the **legacy**
 (A) debt
 (B) inheritance
 (C) question
 (D) lawsuit
 (E) building

____ 6. to be **livid**
 (A) helpful
 (B) dishonest
 (C) furious
 (D) concerned
 (E) enviable

____ 7. to **mortify** someone
 (A) treat unjustly
 (B) give aid to
 (C) shame
 (D) slay
 (E) uphold

____ 8. **patent** falsehoods
 (A) partial
 (B) sly
 (C) common
 (D) obvious
 (E) unknown

____ 9. a famous **patriarch**
 (A) troublemaker
 (B) monument
 (C) song
 (D) adventurer
 (E) founder

____ 10. to **wheedle** a favor
 (A) coax
 (B) grant
 (C) ignore
 (D) request
 (E) receive

24 FORMATIVE ASSESSMENT

Name _____ Date _____ Class _____

USING NEW WORDS ON TESTS

Test 23

Directions. In the space provided, write the letter of the word or phrase closest in meaning to the boldface word. *(10 points each)*

____ 1. to **botch** a job
   (A) want
   (B) finish
   (C) direct
   (D) correct
   (E) spoil

____ 2. helping the **clientele**
   (A) children
   (B) customers
   (C) campaign
   (D) clinic
   (E) government

____ 3. a school **closure**
   (A) playground
   (B) auditorium
   (C) closing
   (D) policy
   (E) teacher

____ 4. to **condole** with a friend
   (A) visit a party
   (B) exchange gifts
   (C) be firm
   (D) mourn in sympathy
   (E) disagree sharply

____ 5. to **convene** a meeting
   (A) attend
   (B) assemble
   (C) dismiss
   (D) criticize
   (E) conduct

____ 6. a **crony** of mine
   (A) friend
   (B) competitor
   (C) story
   (D) relative
   (E) pet

____ 7. **impartial** decisions
   (A) fair
   (B) difficult
   (C) important
   (D) unfair
   (E) unimportant

____ 8. an **indifferent** student
   (A) occasional
   (B) uninterested
   (C) curious
   (D) confident
   (E) undependable

____ 9. gather **momentum**
   (A) force
   (B) pieces
   (C) importance
   (D) votes
   (E) ideas

____ 10. to **stipulate** the rent
   (A) argue over
   (B) raise
   (C) pay on time
   (D) specify
   (E) refuse

USING NEW WORDS ON TESTS **25**

Using New Words on Tests

Test 24

Directions. In the space provided, write the letter of the word or phrase closest in meaning to the boldface word. *(10 points each)*

___ 1. to act as the **arbiter**
   (A) leader
   (B) teacher
   (C) aviator
   (D) judge
   (E) minister

___ 2. a **breach** in the wall
   (A) window
   (B) brick
   (C) treasure
   (D) doorway
   (E) gap

___ 3. to engage in **cant**
   (A) optimistic talk
   (B) truthful talk
   (C) courteous talk
   (D) insincere talk
   (E) boring talk

___ 4. a **disconcerting** situation
   (A) compassionate
   (B) unchangeable
   (C) similar
   (D) fascinating
   (E) embarrassing

___ 5. to keep one's **equilibrium**
   (A) diet
   (B) balance
   (C) health
   (D) innocence
   (E) opinion

___ 6. **oblivious** of the facts
   (A) notified
   (B) unaware
   (C) scornful
   (D) aware
   (E) careful

___ 7. to **rectify** an error
   (A) remedy
   (B) notice
   (C) avoid
   (D) cause
   (E) promote

___ 8. a political **strategem**
   (A) scheme
   (B) candidate
   (C) election
   (D) blunder
   (E) disagreement

___ 9. **subsidiary** topics
   (A) arguable
   (B) principal
   (C) dull
   (D) subordinate
   (E) interesting

___ 10. **substantially** faster service
   (A) somewhat
   (B) always
   (C) significantly
   (D) increasingly
   (E) usually

Using New Words on Tests

Test 25

Directions. In the space provided, write the letter of the word or phrase closest in meaning to the boldface word. *(10 points each)*

____ 1. to **debase** oneself
  (A) raise
  (B) purify
  (C) lower
  (D) move
  (E) lead

____ 2. **effervescent** drinks
  (A) bubbling
  (B) hot
  (C) cold
  (D) sweetened
  (E) spicy

____ 3. to **explicate** the issue
  (A) confuse
  (B) reverse
  (C) ignore
  (D) explain
  (E) forget

____ 4. **immaculate** clothing
  (A) new
  (B) old-fashioned
  (C) dirty-looking
  (D) practical
  (E) spotless

____ 5. the **imposition** of a tax
  (A) late payment penalty
  (B) official lifting
  (C) unreasonable amount
  (D) set by authority
  (E) formal delivery

____ 6. to **mull** over an idea
  (A) argue
  (B) exclaim
  (C) ponder
  (D) agree
  (E) laugh

____ 7. to **quibble** about it
  (A) feel hopeless
  (B) think at length
  (C) feel angry
  (D) find fault
  (E) finally agree

____ 8. a **resonant** bell
  (A) cracked
  (B) resounding
  (C) newly cast
  (D) old-fashioned
  (E) brass

____ 9. **sporadic** noises
  (A) loud
  (B) frequent
  (C) strange
  (D) occasional
  (E) growing

____ 10. a process of **synthesis**
  (A) overcoming opposition to gain a desired end
  (B) making a whole from separate elements
  (C) appealing to the better instincts of
  (D) resolving disagreements
  (E) choosing a person to decide a dispute

Using New Words on Tests

Test 26

Directions. In the space provided, write the letter of the word or phrase closest in meaning to the boldface word. *(10 points each)*

____ 1. to **abdicate** responsibility
 (A) claim
 (B) assume
 (C) give up
 (D) share
 (E) forget

____ 2. the latest **episode**
 (A) fashion
 (B) incident
 (C) opportunity
 (D) model
 (E) thought

____ 3. his **inadvertent** joke
 (A) planned
 (B) bad
 (C) unintentional
 (D) funny
 (E) uninteresting

____ 4. **infallible** judgment
 (A) foolish
 (B) changing
 (C) unreliable
 (D) desired
 (E) reliable

____ 5. to plan her **itinerary**
 (A) route
 (B) party
 (C) meal
 (D) game
 (E) speech

____ 6. their **naive** outlook
 (A) humorous
 (B) pessimistic
 (C) confused
 (D) unsophisticated
 (E) remarkable

____ 7. insults that **rankle** me
 (A) amuse
 (B) interest
 (C) irritate
 (D) confuse
 (E) warn

____ 8. **sardonic** comments
 (A) wise
 (B) scornful
 (C) pleasant
 (D) insincere
 (E) discouraging

____ 9. a heart **stimulant**
 (A) rare disease
 (B) medical specialist
 (C) substance that quickens
 (D) measurement device
 (E) surgical procedure

____ 10. **translucent** windows
 (A) semitransparent
 (B) shaded
 (C) clear
 (D) overhead
 (E) semicircled

Using New Words on Tests

Test 27

Directions. In the space provided, write the letter of the word or phrase closest in meaning to the boldface word. *(10 points each)*

____ 1. a **demure** child
 (A) shameless
 (B) modest
 (C) beautiful
 (D) sassy
 (E) happy

____ 2. to **edify** the public
 (A) criticize
 (B) follow
 (C) praise
 (D) entertain
 (E) instruct

____ 3. **intermittent** rain
 (A) steady
 (B) heavy
 (C) occasional
 (D) seasonal
 (E) freezing

____ 4. **intuition** about a cure
 (A) strange fears
 (B) scientific plan
 (C) sharp insight
 (D) complete ignorance
 (E) false hopes

____ 5. **irrelevant** details
 (A) not important
 (B) not applicable
 (C) not public
 (D) very complicated
 (E) carefully explained

____ 6. a **pallid** face
 (A) pale
 (B) young
 (C) serious
 (D) pleasant
 (E) smooth

____ 7. **redundant** words
 (A) repetitious
 (B) infrequent
 (C) hurtful
 (D) harsh
 (E) pleasant

____ 8. **reminiscent** of the 1940s
 (A) explanatory
 (B) neglectful
 (C) suggestive
 (D) nostalgic
 (E) complimentary

____ 9. wrote the **sequel**
 (A) report
 (B) article
 (C) play
 (D) continuation
 (E) speech

____ 10. wrote a **synopsis**
 (A) poem
 (B) play
 (C) story
 (D) criticism
 (E) summary

USING NEW WORDS ON TESTS

Test 28

Directions. In the space provided, write the letter of the word or phrase closest in meaning to the boldface word. *(10 points each)*

___ 1. to **contend** with the enemy
   (A) negotiate
   (B) be harsh
   (C) be nervous
   (D) battle
   (E) be peaceful

___ 2. to **daunt** the foe
   (A) dismiss
   (B) capture
   (C) scare
   (D) conquer
   (E) blame

___ 3. to **detonate** a mine
   (A) inspect
   (B) locate
   (C) explode
   (D) avoid
   (E) build

___ 4. to **eject** someone
   (A) throw out
   (B) rely upon
   (C) bring in
   (D) confine temporarily
   (E) smile at

___ 5. **irrational** fears
   (A) understandable
   (B) senseless
   (C) nerve-wracking
   (D) short-lived
   (E) horrible

___ 6. to **jostle** someone
   (A) amuse
   (B) please
   (C) anger
   (D) shove
   (E) announce

___ 7. a special **lexicon**
   (A) meal
   (B) culture
   (C) idea
   (D) person
   (E) vocabulary

___ 8. a favorite **rendezvous**
   (A) love song
   (B) meeting place
   (C) fancy dinner
   (D) French restaurant
   (E) evening show

___ 9. to **simulate** an accident
   (A) cause
   (B) imitate
   (C) witness
   (D) avoid
   (E) want

___ 10. a **throng** of memories
   (A) surge
   (B) source
   (C) group
   (D) treasure
   (E) journal

30 FORMATIVE ASSESSMENT

Using New Words on Tests

Test 29

Directions. In the space provided, write the letter of the word or phrase closest in meaning to the boldface word. *(10 points each)*

_____ 1. the **decrepit** house
 (A) broken-down
 (B) small
 (C) old-fashioned
 (D) new
 (E) clean

_____ 2. to enjoy a **farce**
 (A) comedy
 (B) drama
 (C) meal
 (D) trip
 (E) picnic

_____ 3. **inconsistent** behavior
 (A) harmonious
 (B) changeable
 (C) unbelievable
 (D) disloyal
 (E) best

_____ 4. **irksome** tasks
 (A) difficult
 (B) challenging
 (C) ordinary
 (D) rewarding
 (E) irritating

_____ 5. to speak **jargon**
 (A) in a loud voice
 (B) informal English
 (C) in riddles
 (D) a foreign language
 (E) a specialized vocabulary

_____ 6. a **malignant** tumor
 (A) rare type of
 (B) life-threatening
 (C) rapidly growing
 (D) recently removed
 (E) previously unnoticed

_____ 7. **obligatory** visits
 (A) volunteer
 (B) unplanned
 (C) required
 (D) pleasant
 (E) enjoyable

_____ 8. to **parody** a style
 (A) admire
 (B) learn
 (C) establish
 (D) mimic
 (E) support

_____ 9. **pertinent** information
 (A) useless
 (B) surprising
 (C) unessential
 (D) appropriate
 (E) pleasant

_____ 10. to **rebuke** someone
 (A) question
 (B) praise
 (C) fear
 (D) scold
 (E) reveal

Using New Words on Tests

Test 30

Directions. In the space provided, write the letter of the word or phrase closest in meaning to the boldface word. *(10 points each)*

___ 1. to **carp** about it
   (A) insist
   (B) agree
   (C) complain
   (D) forget
   (E) report

___ 2. a **caustic** substance
   (A) bright
   (B) soothing
   (C) mild
   (D) sweet
   (E) corrosive

___ 3. their **coincidental** meeting
   (A) planned
   (B) secret
   (C) public
   (D) accidental
   (E) controversial

___ 4. **incendiary** words
   (A) rebellious
   (B) complimentary
   (C) informal
   (D) calm
   (E) creative

___ 5. **negligible** amounts
   (A) insufficient
   (B) reducible
   (C) insignificant
   (D) specific
   (E) plentiful

___ 6. an **odious** job
   (A) hateful
   (B) pleasant
   (C) necessary
   (D) unimportant
   (E) paid

___ 7. rocks that **protrude**
   (A) obstruct
   (B) project
   (C) injure
   (D) conceal
   (E) crumble

___ 8. to write the **scenario**
   (A) essay
   (B) letter
   (C) novel
   (D) outline
   (E) poem

___ 9. the **sordid** details
   (A) specific
   (B) degrading
   (C) organized
   (D) numerous
   (E) unnecessary

___ 10. an abrupt **transition**
   (A) entrance
   (B) exit
   (C) change
   (D) ending
   (E) decision

Summative Assessment

Tests 1–3

Using New Words on Tests

Test 1 — CONTEXT: Expression

Making New Words Your Own   Lessons 1–10
Connecting New Words and Patterns   Lessons 1–5
Reading New Words in Context   Lessons 1–5

PART A • Critical Reading

Directions. Read the following passage; then circle the letter of the correct answer to each of the twenty items that follow it. The numbers of the items are the same as the numbers of the boldface vocabulary words in the passage. *(1 point each)*

Topic: Confucius in the Classroom

I first got the idea for my term paper when we started reading the sayings of Confucius (551–479 B.C.). I had never heard of Confucius, but I soon found out that he was one of the most famous figures of ancient times. There is no doubt that he was one of the greatest philosophers and teachers in China's **antiquity** (1).

What Did Confucius Teach?
Basically, Confucius was concerned with **ethical** (2) matters—that is, with right and wrong conduct. We learned some of Confucius's teachings by reading passages from the *Analects*, a record of conversations between Confucius and his students. The *Analects* is a group of twenty books that Confucius's followers compiled after his death. Since Confucius didn't write the books himself, they probably don't recreate his conversations **verbatim** (3). Yet the books manage to get across the **postulates** (4), or basic principles, of Confucius's teachings, even if the writers didn't reproduce all of the sayings word for word.

One of my favorite passages is about government. Confucius says, "If there is enough food and if there are enough weapons, the people will put their trust in it." When asked which of these he would be most willing to do without, he replies, "I would give up weapons." In other words, he suggests that military might is of secondary importance—that earning the trust of the people is more important than building up **martial** (5) forces.

Confucius was the first to admit that his teachings were not new, or **unprecedented** (6); rather, they had a basis in Chinese traditions with which educated people of the time would have been familiar. Many of Confucius's sayings seem to be **axioms** (7), or self-evident truths. For example, Confucius said, "Do not inflict on others what you yourself would not wish done to you." That saying has been repeated so many times that it may seem stale and trite to modern-day readers. Yet in Confucius's time, it probably was not a **cliché** (8), and the fact that Confucius's ideas were not totally original doesn't make them any less impressive. Confucius helped his students to interpret and understand ancient wisdom, and he also taught them how to think for themselves.

Confucius at East High?
Reading the conversations from the *Analects*, I could not help thinking that Confucianism is **compatible** (9) with the guidelines of behavior that we are taught to follow today. To

prove that ancient and modern-day wisdom work well together, I decided to write my term paper in the form of a dialogue between Confucius and our class. My sister, who's critical of everything, thought this was an **atrocious** (10) idea, but I didn't think it was horrible at all. True, the scene with the time machine was a bit **melodramatic** (11), but I think that a little sensationalism helps liven up a paper. Besides, our teacher had encouraged us to be creative.

At first I wasn't sure how to portray Confucius. After looking at a seventeenth-century portrait of Confucius, however, I decided to describe him as a pale, feeble-looking man whose **wan** (12) appearance hid a strong, vigorous mind. Since Confucius was often so intent on his teaching that he forgot to eat, I assumed that he was a thin man rather than a **portly** (13) one, although I have seen other portraits that make him look rather stout.

In my report, Confucius visited our class first thing in the morning. He possessed a quiet **aura** (14) of dignity that contrasted with the rowdy manner of students who hadn't yet settled down for the day. However, when we saw Confucius, our **visages** (15) reflected our amazement; we all had awe-struck looks on our faces. Confucius stood close to the front row, and at first, the **proximity** (16) of this great philosopher made us feel a bit nervous.

However, Confucius was so kind and friendly that we soon regained our **composure** (17) and continued calmly with the class.

Each student in the class had an opportunity to ask Confucius for advice. Some students asked general, philosophical questions. For example, Felicia asked, "What's the secret to becoming a better person?" Confucius replied **emphatically** (18), "If he commits a fault, he should not shrink from correcting it." Spoken so forcefully, this simple advice took on great meaning.

I decided to ask a more specific question. "I'm sixteen years old. Do you think I should start thinking about college, or should I wait until next year to worry about it?"

Confucius didn't **grimace** (19), or twist up his face, as if my question were a waste of time. Instead, he thought for a moment and then replied, "If a man take no thought about what is distant, he will find sorrow near at hand." I guess that means I should start reading those college guides after all!

As I wrote the paper, I wondered if Confucius would have minded someone using his sayings in a setting so unfamiliar to him. I like to think that even if he were offended, he would kindly grant me an **acquittal** (20) from charges of using too much creative freedom. He would understand that I only wanted to bring his words into the modern world.

1. In the preceding passage, **antiquity** means
   (A) great philosophers
   (B) recent history
   (C) famous schools
   (D) ancient times
   (E) military government

2. In the preceding passage, **ethical** means
   (A) pertaining to being interesting
   (B) pertaining to right and wrong
   (C) pertaining to learning
   (D) pertaining to listening carefully
   (E) pertaining to enjoyment

3. In the preceding passage, **verbatim** means
   (A) in general
   (B) translated from a foreign language
   (C) word for word
   (D) overheard conversations
   (E) written sayings

4. In the preceding passage, **postulates** means
   (A) ancient philosophies
   (B) great powers
   (C) basic principles
   (D) Chinese sayings
   (E) unstated thoughts

Name _____ Date _____ Class _____

5. In the preceding passage, **martial** means
   (A) terrorist
   (B) secondary
   (C) peaceful
   (D) military
   (E) important

6. In the preceding passage, **unprecedented** means
   (A) frequently happening
   (B) enjoyed greatly
   (C) normal for the time
   (D) traditionally accepted
   (E) unheard of

7. In the preceding passage, **axioms** means
   (A) unfamiliar words
   (B) self-evident truths
   (C) similar meanings
   (D) heroic actions
   (E) simple solutions

8. In the preceding passage, **cliché** means
   (A) original saying
   (B) trite saying
   (C) respected idea
   (D) clever thought
   (E) unusual saying

9. In the preceding passage, **compatible** means
   (A) working well with
   (B) very opposed to
   (C) accustomed to
   (D) in conflict with
   (E) always misunderstood

10. In the preceding passage, **atrocious** means
    (A) creative
    (B) difficult
    (C) critical
    (D) interesting
    (E) horrible

11. In the preceding passage, **melodramatic** means
    (A) awful
    (B) futuristic
    (C) ordinary
    (D) controversial
    (E) sensational

12. In the preceding passage, **wan** means
    (A) pale and feeble
    (B) silent and shy
    (C) healthy and energetic
    (D) strong and healthy
    (E) puzzled and upset

13. In the preceding passage, **portly** means
    (A) strong
    (B) stout
    (C) tall
    (D) thin
    (E) short

14. In the preceding passage, **aura** means
    (A) method
    (B) tone
    (C) quality
    (D) walk
    (E) kindness

15. In the preceding passage, **visages** means
    (A) fears
    (B) reflections
    (C) puzzles
    (D) manners
    (E) faces

16. In the preceding passage, **proximity** means
    (A) closeness
    (B) kindness
    (C) distance
    (D) attraction
    (E) nervousness

17. In the preceding passage, **composure** means
    (A) balance
    (B) excitement
    (C) calmness
    (D) wisdom
    (E) friendliness

18. In the preceding passage, **emphatically** means
    (A) philosophically
    (B) unexcitedly
    (C) simply
    (D) forcefully
    (E) silently

USING NEW WORDS ON TESTS

19. In the preceding passage, **grimace** means
    (A) choose one's words
    (B) talk loudly
    (C) twist one's face
    (D) smile broadly
    (E) shout and wave

20. In the preceding passage, **acquittal** means
    (A) lengthy imprisonment
    (B) official conviction
    (C) informal questioning
    (D) setting free
    (E) final appeal

PART B • Sentence Completion

Directions. For each of the following items, circle the letter of the choice that best completes the meaning of the sentence or sentences. *(1 point each)*

21. During his lifetime, Confucius was honored throughout China as a wise man. He was honored _____ as well, for after his death, temples to him were built in nearly every city of China.
    (A) inarticulately
    (B) melodramatically
    (C) indignantly
    (D) posthumously
    (E) militantly

22. We looked in an encyclopedia to _____ if Confucius was the philosopher's _____ name; we discovered with certainty that it was not.
    (A) fabricate ... first
    (B) deny ... paternal
    (C) discern ... actual
    (D) condescend ... Chinese
    (E) paraphrase ... foreign

23. Because we are on the subject, now is an _____, or fitting, time to tell you that the name Confucius is the European form of the name K'ung Fu-tzu, or Master K'ung.
    (A) amiable
    (B) opportune
    (C) atrocious
    (D) implacable
    (E) elite

24. Confucius, given the name K'ung Ch'iu at birth, was born in the Chinese state of Lu, according to an _____ from a biography that I read.
    (A) axiom
    (B) elite
    (C) affiliate
    (D) excerpt
    (E) impediment

25. Because his father died when Confucius was three years old, the boy grew up without the benefit of _____ advice.
    (A) paternal
    (B) callous
    (C) painstaking
    (D) mutable
    (E) pivotal

26. Confucius was a(n) _____ youth whose actions deserve praise. For example, it's _____ that Confucius worked to help support himself and his mother.
    (A) apprehensive ... lazy
    (B) whimsical ... wild
    (C) responsible ... commendable
    (D) unknown ... portly
    (E) humble ... pompous

27. The young Confucius must have had much _____ because he not only worked for a living but also studied and _____ both music and archery. Still, fatigue must have caught up with him occasionally.
    (A) charisma ... misunderstood
    (B) stamina ... practiced
    (C) nerve ... loathed
    (D) notoriety ... destroyed
    (E) retribution ... loved

28. His love of music and poetry tells us that Confucius was a(n) _____ person who appreciated beauty.
    (A) atrocious
    (B) aesthetic
    (C) painstaking
    (D) indignant
    (E) indestructible

29. Confucius could not have been a _____ person because he valued compassion and kindness above all things.
    (A) zealous
    (B) callous
    (C) compassionate
    (D) judicious
    (E) plausible

30. In an old painting of Confucius, the philosopher is smiling in a friendly manner; he looks quite _____.
    (A) amiable
    (B) callous
    (C) indignant
    (D) pompous
    (E) stringent

31. I would be equally excited to have either the Greek philosopher Socrates or Confucius for a teacher. Both are superior examples of intelligent men given to _____ thinking.
(A) exalted
(B) contemptuous
(C) indignant
(D) insipid
(E) mediocre

32. The Chinese _____ him a master because he was such a good teacher. He had a natural, or _____, ability to teach.
(A) called ... inarticulate
(B) sent ... atrocious
(C) encompassed ... discouraging
(D) elected ... ineffectual
(E) considered ... innate

33. Confucius's _____ of teaching was to encourage students to think for themselves. Apparently, his approach worked; therefore, it was not _____.
(A) system ... martial
(B) recourse ... useful
(C) affiliate ... heresy
(D) method ... ineffectual
(E) proximity ... atrocious

34. Confucius taught his students to be persistent and _____, not easily _____, in their pursuit of wisdom and perfection.
(A) indignant ... incorrect
(B) ineffectual ... whimsical
(C) indomitable ... discouraged
(D) insipid ... despised
(E) prophetic ... apprehensive

35. Confucius rarely taught at schools. Perhaps he did not want to be _____ by rules and _____ that could have interfered with his unique teaching style.
(A) rejuvenated ... mentors
(B) affiliated ... clichés
(C) encumbered ... regulations
(D) helped ... paradoxes
(E) fabricated ... textbooks

36. Traveling and teaching young students may have _____ Confucius—that is, it may have kept him feeling youthful.
(A) deteriorated
(B) succumbed
(C) repressed
(D) postulated
(E) rejuvenated

37. Confucius saw disorder wherever he went; it was _____ in his society.
(A) prophetic
(B) plausible
(C) exalted
(D) prevalent
(E) compassionate

38. The only _____ people had to correct disorder, Confucius felt, was to turn to the principles of the past for guidance.
(A) grimace
(B) recourse
(C) excerpt
(D) recipient
(E) electorate

39. Confucius apparently had a clear _____ of the past, an understanding and insight that is obvious in his historical writings.
(A) antiquity
(B) proximity
(C) perception
(D) recourse
(E) axiom

40. Confucius's strong belief in the value of ancient Chinese customs and _____ of behavior was _____, or central, part of his philosophy.
(A) qualms ... an unknown
(B) impediments ... a deniable
(C) names ... a verbatim
(D) clichés ... a changeable
(E) codes ... a pivotal

Name _____ Date _____ Class _____

41. For a time Confucius was ____ with the state government of Lu, but he ended his association so that he could return to teaching.
    (A) affiliated
    (B) asserted
    (C) repressed
    (D) postulated
    (E) evolved

42. The Confucian gentleman was among the ____ of the land, one of the select government workers who wisely advised the ____ and helped the common people.
    (A) heresy . . . servants
    (B) axiom . . . church
    (C) elite . . . ruler
    (D) outcasts . . . mentors
    (E) antiquity . . . courts

43. As minister of crime, Confucius showed the moral courage, or ____, to make ____ reforms and to fight crime.
    (A) compassion . . . unnecessary
    (B) cowardice . . . posthumous
    (C) fortitude . . . necessary
    (D) personification . . . judicious
    (E) meanness . . . whimsical

44. Under Confucius, people who disobeyed laws were dealt with justly. Those who were not in ____ with the laws ____ fair punishments.
    (A) recourse . . . demanded
    (B) paradox . . . discerned
    (C) perception . . . conceived
    (D) compliance . . . received
    (E) impediment . . . excerpted

45. Confucius believed a ruler should have ____ for his subjects; such a ruler would have sympathy for people's conditions and a desire to help them.
    (A) compassion
    (B) charisma
    (C) heresy
    (D) notoriety
    (E) retribution

46. The ideal Confucian ruler would feel anger at injustice and thus would be ____ if any of his people were ____ unfairly.
    (A) contemptuous . . . loved
    (B) exalted . . . conceived
    (C) insipid . . . working
    (D) indignant . . . treated
    (E) inanimate . . . loathed

47. Confucius and his wife had three children; his wife ____ one boy and two girls.
    (A) condescended
    (B) conceived
    (C) repressed
    (D) discerned
    (E) encumbered

48. In Confucius's view, the ideal gentleman would not consider it beneath his dignity to take care of everyday matters. Thus, he would not tend to his family and the ____ of his household in a(n) ____ way.
    (A) aura . . . martial
    (B) recourse . . . polite
    (C) compassion . . . ethical
    (D) details . . . condescending
    (E) acquittal . . . verbatim

49. Do you think that Confucius's concept of the relationship of family and government is ____, or do you think it seems unlikely and untrue?
    (A) contemptuous
    (B) prolific
    (C) painstaking
    (D) atrocious
    (E) plausible

50. Confucius strongly stated a central belief of his when he ____ that the government could be run well if all families also were ____ well.
    (A) asserted . . . managed
    (B) repressed . . . doing
    (C) denied . . . rejuvenated
    (D) evolved . . . kept
    (E) thought . . . encumbered

51. Did the ideas of Confucius seem like ____ to philosophers who supported older, more accepted doctrines?
(A) heresy
(B) composure
(C) evolution
(D) compatibility
(E) visages

52. Confucius had many suggestions for how to become a better person. Some people may consider these methods too ____, or strict, and may say they are unable to live by the code of conduct that Confucius ____.
(A) commendable ... asserted
(B) atrocious ... enjoyed
(C) compassionate ... evolved
(D) stringent ... promoted
(E) inarticulate ... preached

53. Others, of course, may have no doubts at all about Confucius's philosophy and may not understand someone else's ____.
(A) lament
(B) compliance
(C) heresy
(D) composure
(E) qualms

54. In Confucian philosophy, what are the ____ for proper human behavior? Confucius ____ that love and goodness were important motivations for most people.
(A) incentives ... believed
(B) analogies ... denied
(C) repressions ... thought
(D) auras ... preached
(E) recipients ... sang

55. True followers of Confucius had to be ____ in their quest for self-discipline and equally relentless in their pursuit of ____ strength.
(A) contemptuous ... physical
(B) melodramatic ... quiet
(C) portly ... great
(D) callous ... immoral
(E) implacable ... moral

56. Over the years, the ideas of Confucius ____ into a philosophy called Confucianism, which has been a major ____ in China.
(A) paraphrased ... disappointment
(B) evolved ... influence
(C) deteriorated ... impediment
(D) disappeared ... heresy
(E) affiliated ... zephyr

57. Confucianism is not a(n) ____ religion, and Confucius has never been regarded as a religious leader or a ____.
(A) unprecedented ... ruler
(B) paradoxical ... minister
(C) established ... mystic
(D) recipient ... elder
(E) presidential ... mystic

58. Some people might find it a(n) ____ that Confucianism promotes what we call religious ideals—honesty, good conduct, and justice—but is not considered a religion.
(A) excerpt
(B) lament
(C) paradox
(D) recourse
(E) analogy

59. During the Han dynasty (206 B.C.–A.D. 220), examinations for government offices ____ Confucian philosophy. Since the official philosophy included elements of Confucianism, candidates for government jobs were ____ to know Confucius's teachings in order to be hired.
(A) affiliated ... forbidden
(B) rejected ... rejuvenated
(C) destroyed ... transcended
(D) inarticulated ... surprised
(E) encompassed ... required

60. The Han dynasty fell and the ____ of Buddhism and Taoism became popular, but Confucianism didn't die; it was ____.
(A) composure ... invisible
(B) philosophies ... indestructible
(C) axiom ... identical
(D) incentive ... whimsical
(E) recourse ... exalted

61. Throughout its various dynasties, Chinese society was subject to change, but the basic principles of Confucianism were stable and not ____.
    (A) inanimate
    (B) ethical
    (C) painstaking
    (D) mutable
    (E) verbatim

62. During the T'ang dynasty (618–907), many scholars must have been aggressive, even ____, in their promotion of Confucianism, because the philosophy prospered and eventually became the official ____ of the state.
    (A) apprehensive . . . religion
    (B) pivotal . . . flag
    (C) militant . . . teaching
    (D) mediocre . . . seal
    (E) pompous . . . education

63. Confucianism ____ the limits of China's borders. Its teachings have spread to Japan, Korea, Indochina, and even to Europe and the United States.
    (A) transcends
    (B) succumbs
    (C) deteriorates
    (D) laments
    (E) represses

64. Since Confucius himself wrote little, he cannot be considered a ____ author.
    (A) prolific
    (B) callous
    (C) paternal
    (D) mediocre
    (E) mystical

65. Sayings of Confucius are ____ included in books of quotations, so you can be certain that you'll find some of the sayings in any library.
    (A) contemptuously
    (B) indignantly
    (C) emphatically
    (D) wanly
    (E) invariably

66. I wish that you would ____ some of the statements by the followers of Confucius because the original wording is ____ for me to understand.
    (A) erase . . . insipid
    (B) evolve . . . mediocre
    (C) paraphrase . . . difficult
    (D) fabricate . . . commendable
    (E) sing . . . apprehensive

67. I tried to read the Analects—collections of Confucius's sayings and his disciples' comments—while vacationing in a log cabin on a ____ of Caddo Lake in East Texas.
    (A) visage
    (B) grimace
    (C) postulate
    (D) zephyr
    (E) bayou

68. The reviewer said the new book about Confucianism was neither very good nor horribly bad; it was merely ____.
    (A) elite
    (B) mediocre
    (C) inanimate
    (D) contemptuous
    (E) inarticulate

69. The writer did point out the difference between real events in Confucius's early life and legends that were ____ later. For example, she explained that someone invented the fanciful story that Confucius's mother was guarded by dragons when he was born.
    (A) asserted
    (B) loathed
    (C) fabricated
    (D) encompassed
    (E) grimaced

70. Although the writer made a few interesting points, the Confucius biography on the whole was as dull and spiritless as a rock or other ____ object.
    (A) exalted
    (B) posthumous
    (C) malleable
    (D) amiable
    (E) inanimate

Using New Words on Tests

Name _____ Date _____ Class _____

PART C • Analogies

Directions. For each of the following items, choose the lettered pair of words that expresses a relationship that is most similar to the relationship between the pair of capitalized words. Write the letter of your answer on the line provided before the number of the item. *(1 point each)*

____ 71. ADORE : LIKE ::
  (A) paraphrase : explain
  (B) assert : deny
  (C) love : learn
  (D) invigorate : invest
  (E) loathe : dislike

____ 72. ANALOGY : COMPARISON ::
  (A) joke : laugh
  (B) noise : silence
  (C) similarity : sameness
  (D) teacher : book
  (E) century : decade

____ 73. APPREHENSIVE : CALM ::
  (A) nervous : nervy
  (B) atrocious : bad
  (C) cool : cold
  (D) tranquil : stormy
  (E) melodramatic : weeping

____ 74. BUYER : SELLER ::
  (A) proximity : touch
  (B) receipt : purchase
  (C) recipient : donor
  (D) visage : mouth
  (E) recess : judge

____ 75. CAREFUL : CAUTIOUS ::
  (A) contemptuous : scornful
  (B) brotherly : fatherly
  (C) intelligent : ethical
  (D) wan : healthy
  (E) confused : changed

____ 76. CHARISMA : CHARM ::
  (A) violinist : music
  (B) talent : ability
  (C) lizard : desert
  (D) smile : frown
  (E) winter : snow

____ 77. DETERIORATE : IMPROVE ::
  (A) ascertain : determine
  (B) succeed : fail
  (C) condescend : agree
  (D) organize : classify
  (E) teethe : bite

____ 78. ELECTORATE : VOTE ::
  (A) bread : bake
  (B) basketball : throw
  (C) winner : lose
  (D) audience : applaud
  (E) dancer : dive

____ 79. IMPEDIMENT : OBSTACLE ::
  (A) foot : tie
  (B) axioms : lies
  (C) device : machine
  (D) grimace : unhappiness
  (E) conservation : energy

____ 80. INARTICULATE : MUTE ::
  (A) think : dissent
  (B) late : sleepy
  (C) energetic : healthy
  (D) shiny : dull
  (E) willing : eager

____ 81. INSIPID : FLAVORLESS ::
  (A) active : listless
  (B) amazing : astonishing
  (C) ecstatic : fortunate
  (D) portly : slim
  (E) countless : worthless

____ 82. JUDICIOUS : UNWISE ::
  (A) sneaky : sly
  (B) unhappy : miserable
  (C) hopeful : wishful
  (D) skillful : crafty
  (E) trustworthy : unreliable

____ 83. LAMENT : MOURNER ::
   (A) pay : baby sitter
   (B) dream : sleeper
   (C) whistle : visitor
   (D) mow : grass
   (E) repair : faucet

____ 84. MALLEABLE : CLAY ::
   (A) flexible : rubber
   (B) posthumous : conclusion
   (C) light : iron
   (D) stretched : antiquity
   (E) soft : marble

____ 85. MENTOR : ADVISE ::
   (A) physician : strike
   (B) dog : encumber
   (C) paradox : mislead
   (D) critic : review
   (E) chord : strike

____ 86. NOTORIETY : FAME ::
   (A) expense : money
   (B) merit : worth
   (C) mediocrity : brilliance
   (D) smile : grimace
   (E) fortune : publicity

____ 87. PERSONIFICATION : FIGURE OF SPEECH ::
   (A) grape : cluster
   (B) bat : baseball
   (C) desk : pencil
   (D) comparison : likeness
   (E) sneaker : footwear

____ 88. POMPOUS : HUMBLE ::
   (A) compassionate : pitiful
   (B) crucial : important
   (C) mutable : changing
   (D) knowledgeable : ignorant
   (E) troubled : terrible

____ 89. PROPHETIC : PREDICTIVE ::
   (A) prosperous : poor
   (B) fabricated : true
   (C) remarkable : outstanding
   (D) compliant : lawless
   (E) dangerous : scared

____ 90. REACTIONARY : REACT ::
   (A) potato : bake
   (B) leaves : shed
   (C) conductor : assert
   (D) novelist : write
   (E) trees : encircle

____ 91. REPRESS : RESTRAIN ::
   (A) give : accept
   (B) bicker : quarrel
   (C) invite : insist
   (D) whisper : urge
   (E) expect : remember

____ 92. RETRIBUTION : WRONGDOING ::
   (A) patience : virtue
   (B) wages : work
   (C) melodrama : tragedy
   (D) mystic : philosophy
   (E) reward : sheriff

____ 93. THREATEN : TERRORIST ::
   (A) acquit : witness
   (B) jog : driver
   (C) argue : lawyer
   (D) encompass : limbs
   (E) plan : date

____ 94. THRILLING : PARACHUTING ::
   (A) commendable : wishing
   (B) tense : relaxing
   (C) painstaking : embroidering
   (D) indignant : forgiving
   (E) painful : swinging

____ 95. TRANSITORY : MOMENT ::
   (A) cold : ice
   (B) curious : investigation
   (C) boiling : heat
   (D) chilly : sweater
   (E) boring : magician

____ 96. VIBRANT : LIFELESS ::
   (A) hesitant : unsure
   (B) changeless : monotonous
   (C) polite : endurable
   (D) restless : uneasy
   (E) vague : clear

USING NEW WORDS ON TESTS

____ 97. WAITER : SERVE ::
(A) bag : rip
(B) orphan : adopt
(C) pauper : beg
(D) excerpt : read
(E) incentive : receive

____ 98. WHIMSICAL : FANCIFUL ::
(A) opportune : inappropriate
(B) approachable : shy
(C) odd : normal
(D) elite : small
(E) tired : weary

____ 99. ZEALOUS : UNENTHUSIASTIC ::
(A) notorious : famous
(B) taxed : wealthy
(C) strong : mighty
(D) ecstatic : pleasant
(E) timid : courageous

____ 100. ZEPHYR : GENTLE ::
(A) breeze : harsh
(B) qualms : worried
(C) researcher : lost
(D) bird : feathered
(E) kite : bulky

Using New Words on Tests

Test 2 — **CONTEXT:** Civilization

Making New Words Your Own   Lessons 11–20
Connecting New Words and Patterns   Lessons 6–10
Reading New Words in Context   Lessons 6–10

PART A • Critical Reading

Directions. Read the following passage; then circle the letter of the correct answer to each of the twenty items that follow it. The numbers of the items are the same as the numbers of the boldface vocabulary words in the passage. *(1 point each)*

Topic: An Early African Society

It was Thursday night, and I still had two important items on my "to do" list. One was to make some **hors d'oeuvres** (1), or appetizers, for a class lunch party. The other was a **mandatory** (2) assignment for my world history class, a required paper on some aspect of ancient African empires. The first task was easy: I'd just slice up some fresh vegetables. The second task, however, was not so easy, and I was beginning to wish that I hadn't put it off until the last minute. Because I'd waited so long to start the assignment, I'd spent a lot of time at the library that afternoon looking for books on my topic. I'd ended up feeling pretty desperate, and, as I feverishly searched the library stacks for usable material, I must have looked like a spy engaged in undercover **espionage** (3) work, racing against the clock to uncover a valuable government secret. Finally, I found a few books that looked helpful.

A Creative Approach

I **commenced** (4) my research by paging through the books I'd checked out. My ancestors were from West Africa, so I began by looking for any information on West Africa that might be interesting to write about. I was pretty proud of my **perseverance** (5); I was persistent and read with concentration for quite a long time. I soon **perceived** (6), though, that I would have to come up with a specific and limited topic quickly, for I observed that there was far more information than I could easily read.

My teacher had mentioned that we could fulfill the assignment in a very creative way: We could write a story or a play, as long as we made sure that we presented plenty of solid information on the topic. I was **astute** (7) enough to realize that she would never let me submit a paper that was merely creative, not grounded in solid facts; and I was clever enough to see that there was a way I could write a good paper and have some fun at the same time. I was very glad that my teacher had given us the **autonomy** (8) to handle the assignment the way we saw fit; that kind of independence is good for creativity, I think. And since I've always loved writing stories, I decided that writing a fictional story instead of writing a dry, factual report was the best way for me to approach my topic.

I don't know how other people write stories, but I usually begin by freewriting, often by holding a "conversation" with an imaginary character. I don't always know where my characters come from—who really understands the creative process anyway?—but I know that writing dialogue really works for me. I'm sometimes amazed at the characters my imagination creates.

I started freewriting, and, before I knew it, I had a character firmly in my mind—a tall, handsome army officer from the ancient kingdom of Ghana in West Africa, sometime before A.D. 1500. I had been reading about Ghana and was particularly impressed with some of the information I had learned. As I conversed on paper with my imaginary army officer friend, it seemed as though he came to life: If I had looked up from my paper and had seen him standing across the room from me, I don't think I would have been surprised. Here's a portion of the "dialogue" I held with him.

A Personal View of History

"Sir, I want to be able to describe the world you lived in—to give my readers the feeling that they're getting a personal, firsthand view of the ancient kingdom of Ghana. What can you tell me?"

"First of all, understand that I lived during the time that was the peak, the very **zenith** (9), of ancient Ghana's power. Those were glorious days. We—the king's palace troops—were **invincible** (10); we could not be conquered by any foe. We were a thousand strong and well armed. We would **annihilate** (11) anyone who tried to harm our beloved king, and we would also destroy anyone who threatened the royal family."

"Tell me about your king. What was he like?"

"Our king was very powerful, and he was the exact opposite of a **pacifist** (12), someone opposed to war. In fact, we called him Ghana, which means "war chief." His armies **ravaged** (13) many towns and small kingdoms; they demolished the cities utterly. The survivors of these attacks were accepted into our society. From then on they were in complete **submission** (14) to the king—completely loyal and obedient to him."

"It sounds like your king ruled mainly through force."

"Not at all. Our king was a strong ruler, but a just and wise one. He ran the kingdom with the help of a council of ministers. He also tried court cases; his court was in Kumbi."

"Did anyone ever challenge your king's power?"

"The king's power was absolute. Everyone acknowledged that his power could neither be given nor taken away—that it was his **inalienable** (15) right to rule us."

"I suppose the king lived in luxury."

"Yes. He was very rich because he controlled the country's gold mines. Ghana is, after all, the land of gold. You should have seen the interior of the king's **ornate** (16) palace, adorned with countless gold decorations. The king himself was often as elaborately decorated as the palace; he and members of the royal family often wore large amounts of beautiful gold jewelry."

"I've read that about 200,000 people lived in your kingdom of Ghana. Obviously, Ghana wasn't a **diminutive** (17) kingdom; in fact, it was larger than many of the other African kingdoms. Did it seem crowded to you?"

"Yes, there were many people living in Ghana then, and many other people came and went, trading goods from other kingdoms. It was an exciting time."

"Earlier, I got the idea that maybe Ghana saw a lot of discord. It seemed like you mentioned wars and battles quite a bit. Was it a violent society during your time?"

"No more so than any other part of the world. Overall, I think you would have found Ghana to be a pleasant, peaceful place. Farming was important throughout Ghana, so as you traveled through the country you would see many peaceful **pastoral** (18) settings—rural scenery of farms, crops, and cattle. People irrigated their crops and bred domestic animals. We were an active society, full of merchants, miners, and cattle breeders, as well as many people with special **aptitudes** (19) for crafts. My mother, for example, had a wonderful natural ability to weave beautiful cloth."

"Sounds great. How did you end up in the king's army?"

I wanted to see the rest of Africa. As soon as I was old enough, I joined the army. I've never regretted it."

48 SUMMATIVE ASSESSMENT, TEST 2

"Did you marry?"

"Actually, I had hoped to marry one of the king's daughters. We were in love, but, as you might guess, a relationship between a member of royalty and a commoner is **precarious** (20), full of uncertainty and danger. It didn't work out, so I didn't end up marrying into the royal family. But I eventually did marry a wonderful, kind woman, and we had six children together."

"I'll bet your life story would make a great historical novel."

"Perhaps. I think that people are more interested in hearing about the lives of individuals than in hearing impersonal facts from a history book. My life in Ghana was certainly very interesting, and you won't read about it in any history text."

"Maybe not, but my teacher and the rest of the class will read about it—because I'm writing it up for my history assignment."

I finished my dialogue and started putting it into narrative form. I can't help but think that one day I might carry my army officer's story still further. Who knows? You might see a historical novel about the ancient kingdom of Ghana at your local bookstore one of these days.

1. In the preceding passage, **hors d'oeuvres** means
   - (A) festive decorations
   - (B) desserts
   - (C) horse feed
   - (D) bakeries
   - (E) appetizers

2. In the preceding passage, **mandatory** means
   - (A) unnecessary
   - (B) required
   - (C) manageable
   - (D) voluntary
   - (E) factual

3. In the preceding passage, **espionage** means
   - (A) excitement
   - (B) government
   - (C) privacy
   - (D) publicity
   - (E) spying

4. In the preceding passage, **commenced** means
   - (A) commented on
   - (B) started
   - (C) rejected
   - (D) finished
   - (E) tightly controlled

5. In the preceding passage, **perseverance** means
   - (A) presence
   - (B) thoughtfulness
   - (C) persistence
   - (D) anger
   - (E) stability

6. In the preceding passage, **perceived** means
   - (A) denied
   - (B) pretended
   - (C) observed
   - (D) recorded
   - (E) hoped

7. In the preceding passage, **astute** means
   - (A) ancient
   - (B) fierce
   - (C) personal
   - (D) clever
   - (E) talkative

8. In the preceding passage, **autonomy** means
   - (A) pride
   - (B) history
   - (C) independence
   - (D) trade
   - (E) interference

USING NEW WORDS ON TESTS

9. In the preceding passage, **zenith** means
   (A) peak
   (B) depth
   (C) sanity
   (D) inside
   (E) outside

10. In the preceding passage, **invincible** means
    (A) conquerable
    (B) invisible
    (C) unconquerable
    (D) unchangeable
    (E) changeable

11. In the preceding passage, **annihilate** means
    (A) protect
    (B) destroy
    (C) question
    (D) confuse
    (E) surrender

12. In the preceding passage, **pacifist** means
    (A) someone who rules like a tyrant
    (B) someone who is traditional
    (C) someone who is a powerful soldier
    (D) someone who is opposed to war
    (E) someone who is flexible

13. In the preceding passage, **ravaged** means
    (A) helped
    (B) moved
    (C) revealed
    (D) enjoyed
    (E) demolished

14. In the preceding passage, **submission** means
    (A) control
    (B) imagination
    (C) creation
    (D) obedience
    (E) resistance

15. In the preceding passage, **inalienable** means
    (A) not capable of being given or taken away
    (B) not capable of being seen or understood
    (C) capable of being controlled
    (D) pertaining to customs of royalty
    (E) having to do with ancient African kingdoms

16. In the preceding passage, **ornate** means
    (A) simple
    (B) gold
    (C) ancient
    (D) elaborate
    (E) plain

17. In the preceding passage, **diminutive** means
    (A) dim
    (B) small
    (C) large
    (D) bright
    (E) crowded

18. In the preceding passage, **pastoral** means
    (A) rural
    (B) religious
    (C) crowded
    (D) comical
    (E) barren

19. In the preceding passage, **aptitudes** means
    (A) absolute powers
    (B) natural abilities
    (C) violent allergies
    (D) secret documents
    (E) dangerous occupations

20. In the preceding passage, **precarious** means
    (A) certain and appealing
    (B) envied and praised
    (C) well accepted and liked
    (D) violent and discouraging
    (E) uncertain and dangerous

Name _____ Date _____ Class _____

PART B • Sentence Completion

Directions. For each of the following items, circle the letter of the choice that best completes the meaning of the sentence or sentences. *(1 point each)*

21. People always have been ____ for rainfall in the dry areas of Africa, partly because they never know when it will ____, or come again.
    (A) vigilant ... censure
    (B) destitute ... lapse
    (C) flagrant ... overflow
    (D) thankful ... recur
    (E) resentful ... obliterate

22. The midwestern senator from the nation's "breadbasket" reminded her ____, who voted for her last month, that Africa was one of the places where agriculture began.
    (A) clemency
    (B) protocol
    (C) autonomy
    (D) constituents
    (E) facsimile

23. The agricultural ____ of African farmers in 1500 B.C. no doubt would look ____ to modern farmers.
    (A) latitude ... exciting
    (B) influx ... frightening
    (C) methods ... archaic
    (D) teaching ... ornate
    (E) autonomy ... simple

24. If you think bananas are delicious, you may be interested to learn that many early African societies grew this ____ fruit.
    (A) mandatory
    (B) flagrant
    (C) meager
    (D) diminutive
    (E) delectable

25. Agricultural conditions in some parts of Africa were not appropriate for growing more juicy or ____ fruit such as oranges.
    (A) succulent
    (B) colloquial
    (C) timorous
    (D) balmy
    (E) tawny

26. To us, certain root crops ____ by early African societies might not seem ____.
    (A) detested ... conducive
    (B) curtailed ... modern
    (C) enjoyed ... palatable
    (D) grown ... astute
    (E) burned ... pastoral

27. As you might expect, Africa's ____ Valley, an early agricultural site, was named for a split in the earth.
    (A) Ornate
    (B) Rift
    (C) Balmy
    (D) Steppe
    (E) Wreak

28. As early as 1000 B.C., ____ discovered that the Senegal River and Lake Chad in the western Sudan were rich with fish and thus ____ to fishing.
    (A) canines ... used
    (B) espionage ... beguiled
    (C) people ... conducive
    (D) pirates ... meager
    (E) travelers ... palatable

29. You can guess what ____ when the Phoenicians introduced ironworking to Africa shortly after 1000 B.C.: The knowledge ____ rapidly throughout the African continent.
    (A) ensued ... spread
    (B) ossified ... expanded
    (C) appeared ... waned
    (D) lapsed ... disappeared
    (E) beguiled ... evaporated

30. ____ trans-Saharan trade routes developed between A.D. 200 and 700. By the fourteenth century, ____, or crossroads, along the routes were very busy with traders.
    (A) Vulnerable ... musicians
    (B) Invincible ... retainers
    (C) Important ... junctures
    (D) Diminutive ... giants
    (E) Major ... rifts

31. Travelers across the Sahara discovered that it was ____, or advantageous, to have camels carry heavy items.
    (A) astute
    (B) requisite
    (C) defunct
    (D) erratic
    (E) expedient

32. The guide's camel behaved ____, but the other camels acted in a foul manner as the supplies were unloaded after the long journey.
    (A) cruelly
    (B) insolently
    (C) vigilantly
    (D) admirably
    (E) timorously

33. These trade routes ____ the growth of African cities, which in turn assisted the development of craft industries.
    (A) purged
    (B) facilitated
    (C) appeased
    (D) beguiled
    (E) censured

34. The ____ to the Kwanzaa celebration was a jazz performance. After this opening, we were shown a film about the African kingdoms and empires of A.D. 800 to 1450.
    (A) prelude
    (B) affidavit
    (C) juncture
    (D) diversion
    (E) pretext

35. The historian who introduced the film did not ____ my question. She told us quite directly that the ancient African kingdoms ____ Ghana, Mali, Ethiopia, and Great Zimbabwe.
    (A) ravage . . . are
    (B) subsidize . . . weren't
    (C) perceive . . . destroyed
    (D) besiege . . . emancipated
    (E) evade . . . included

36. The original Soninke people of Ghana were joined by an ____ of Muslim traders; other foreigners also came into Ghana at that time.
    (A) amnesty
    (B) inhibition
    (C) innovation
    (D) influx
    (E) edifice

37. The large Muslim ____ in Ghana had as many as twelve mosques. I wonder how high the ____ of the tallest mosque was.
    (A) juncture . . . buffet
    (B) foundation . . . defunct
    (C) community . . . apex
    (D) steppe . . . coffer
    (E) retainer . . . latitude

38. Do you think mosques in Africa today are new designs or ____ of mosques from long ago?
    (A) affidavits
    (B) hieroglyphics
    (C) facsimiles
    (D) zeniths
    (E) retainers

39. One can imagine that the leaders of the kingdoms bordering Ghana were not merely ____, they were completely intimidated. After all, Ghana's thousands of soldiers—many armed with bows and arrows—must have been frightening to the neighboring countries.
    (A) astute
    (B) timorous
    (C) invincible
    (D) meticulous
    (E) defunct

40. Small African kingdoms probably tried unsuccessfully to ____ Ghana's "war chief," who ____ demanded that they give in to him.
    (A) appease . . . continually
    (B) dissent . . . never
    (C) capture . . . admirably
    (D) beguile . . . sweetly
    (E) facilitate . . . cruelly

Name _____ Date _____ Class _____

41. I am afraid that many of Ghana's "war chiefs" _____ vengeance on their enemies and severely punished the survivors of their attacks.
    (A) subsidized
    (B) lapsed
    (C) commenced
    (D) wreaked
    (E) waned

42. It seems doubtful to me that the Ghanaian rulers took _____ political prisoners. If they did, it is unlikely that they granted _____ to any of them and set them free.
    (A) exultant ... censure
    (B) astute ... freedom
    (C) flagrant ... knighthood
    (D) colloquial ... degrees
    (E) many ... amnesty

43. Sundiata (?–1255) _____ the forces of Sumanguru in the Battle of Kirina in 1235. By destroying Sumanguru's forces, Sundiata freed the state of Kangaba from Ghana.
    (A) purged
    (B) wreaked
    (C) decimated
    (D) dissented
    (E) consolidated

44. Sumanguru was the last ruler of the now _____ Ghana Empire. The destruction of Sumanguru's forces virtually ended the empire of Ghana.
    (A) evaded
    (B) delayed
    (C) requisite
    (D) appeased
    (E) defunct

45. After Ghana divided into several small kingdoms, the political climate became _____ as violent disturbances developed.
    (A) balmy
    (B) archaic
    (C) inalienable
    (D) inclement
    (E) decimated

46. Eventually, one people, the Mandinke, joined together to _____ their _____ and resources to form the kingdom of Mali around A.D. 1200 to 1450.
    (A) dissent ... royalty
    (B) besiege ... memories
    (C) consolidate ... forces
    (D) destroy ... autonomy
    (E) emancipate ... canines

47. In the thirteenth century, Mali rulers must have been _____, rejoicing over the kingdom's success.
    (A) defunct
    (B) bourgeois
    (C) vulnerable
    (D) exultant
    (E) erratic

48. Mali was certainly not a _____ force in West African trade; it had many companies and traders and much influence.
    (A) mandatory
    (B) meticulous
    (C) meager
    (D) requisite
    (E) dissenting

49. Mali farmers were very successful. Food supplies _____, and the population grew and _____.
    (A) curtailed ... celebrated
    (B) matured ... rebelled
    (C) subsidized ... voted
    (D) decimated ... profited
    (E) abounded ... prospered

50. Enemies found it impossible to _____ the growing power of the Mali ruler Mansa Musa (ca. 1312–1337); his power increased with every military victory.
    (A) beguile
    (B) bias
    (C) decimate
    (D) perceive
    (E) curtail

USING NEW WORDS ON TESTS 53

51. From what I have read, Mansa Musa was a skilled _____ who made certain that his soldiers were protected. His troops, heavily armed, were not _____ in battle.
(A) rivulet . . . seen
(B) mosque . . . injured
(C) warrior . . . vulnerable
(D) constituent . . . excited
(E) retainer . . . recognized

52. Rulers such as Mansa Musa certainly would not have tolerated any _____ from their servants or any disrespect from their soldiers.
(A) insolence
(B) aptitude
(C) concession
(D) submission
(E) perseverance

53. An _____ in African government was Mansa Musa's new practice of naming members of the royal family to govern _____, or outer regions.
(A) influx . . . children
(B) amnesty . . . themselves
(C) inhibition . . . wisely
(D) innovation . . . provinces
(E) affidavit . . . slaves

54. Mansa Musa had no _____ about showing off his empire's gold and other riches. He certainly showed no restraint in his visit to Cairo, Egypt, where he made no attempt to hide his _____.
(A) inhibitions . . . wealth
(B) perseverance . . . letters
(C) protocol . . . lessons
(D) requisites . . . autonomy
(E) submission . . . dedication

55. The rulers of these early African kingdoms and empires apparently observed a special set of rules or _____, especially when they were _____ meeting other rulers.
(A) holidays . . . erratically
(B) submission . . . admirably
(C) ultimatums . . . peacefully
(D) amnesty . . . angrily
(E) protocol . . . officially

56. Mansa Musa was accompanied by hundreds of _____. Among them were five hundred slaves who came before him and carried gold rods.
(A) canines
(B) edifices
(C) retainers
(D) junctures
(E) mannerisms

57. Evidently, Mansa Musa used every _____, or excuse, available to flaunt his riches.
(A) latitude
(B) pretext
(C) juncture
(D) edifice
(E) zenith

58. The emperor's _____ behavior in Egypt included especially outrageous acts of giving away large sums of gold.
(A) bourgeois
(B) expedient
(C) vigilant
(D) ornate
(E) flagrant

59. Mansa Musa presumably was not trying to _____ anyone. He had no reason to deceive others about his great fortune.
(A) censure
(B) beguile
(C) appease
(D) ossify
(E) curtail

60. Giving away gold probably was just a _____ for Mansa Musa. But though the gesture may have been nothing more than a game he used to amuse himself, a writer of the time _____ that the act "ruined the value of money" in Cairo.
(A) censure . . . applauded
(B) pretext . . . decimated
(C) ultimatum . . . perceived
(D) diversion . . . noted
(E) prelude . . . purged

Name _____ Date _____ Class _____

61. Who could _____ Mansa Musa for letting the world know about his wealthy country? Though some might be critical, the fact remained that from then on the world looked upon Mali as a(n) _____ empire.
    (A) besiege . . . defunct
    (B) censure . . . mighty
    (C) ensue . . . erratic
    (D) commence . . . meager
    (E) appease . . . foreign

62. As a Muslim, the emperor _____ the building of new mosques, donating large amounts of money. He also promoted the wearing of Muslim clothes by Malian traders and merchants.
    (A) beguiled
    (B) evaded
    (C) subsidized
    (D) recurred
    (E) ravaged

63. Under Mansa Musa, Timbuktu's importance did not _____; rather, it grew into a large, successful commercial center.
    (A) wane
    (B) wreak
    (C) purge
    (D) besiege
    (E) obliterate

64. The Aksum Kingdom, the ancestor of Ethiopia, was the commercial _____ of East Africa. Its diverse population must have ranged from wealthy merchants to _____ families.
    (A) facsimile . . . rich
    (B) edifice . . . broken
    (C) envy . . . erratic
    (D) center . . . destitute
    (E) pacifist . . . banking

65. In the 600s, Aksum's power _____ after Muslims gained control of nearby areas, including the Red Sea. This sudden fall of power put an end to the kingdom's foreign trade.
    (A) purged
    (B) evaded
    (C) lapsed
    (D) ossified
    (E) recurred

66. It was not easy for some travelers to reach Ethiopia because the country's rugged mountains made it nearly _____.
    (A) pastoral
    (B) erratic
    (C) mandatory
    (D) bedlam
    (E) inaccessible

67. The early African societies that prospered changed with the times and did not make the mistake of becoming rigid, or _____.
    (A) ossified
    (B) vigilant
    (C) invincible
    (D) pastoral
    (E) quantitative

68. One _____ to becoming a successful merchant in the kingdom of Ethiopia was to establish _____ contacts with the Romans. These contacts were absolutely necessary.
    (A) pretext . . . flagrant
    (B) bias . . . illegal
    (C) concession . . . silent
    (D) requisite . . . trading
    (E) diversion . . . colloquial

69. Are the ruins of Great Zimbabwe, in South Africa, which include dry-stone buildings and walls, _____ or tan like the color of sand?
    (A) ossified
    (B) palatable
    (C) tawny
    (D) pastoral
    (E) ornate

70. Archaeologists must be _____ in order to find important information. For example, alert archaeologists _____ evidence that gold and copper decorations originally were on the buildings.
    (A) flagrant . . . ravaged
    (B) mandatory . . . overlooked
    (C) vigilant . . . discovered
    (D) exultant . . . ignored
    (E) wise . . . facilitated

Name _____ Date _____ Class _____

Part C • Analogies

Directions. For each of the following items, choose the lettered pair of words that expresses a relationship that is most similar to the relationship between the pair of capitalized words. Write the letter of your answer on the line provided before the number of the item. *(1 point each)*

____ 71. AFFIDAVIT : WITNESS ::
  (A) hospital : patient
  (B) coffer : cushion
  (C) furniture : chair
  (D) law : legislators
  (E) mason : buffet

____ 72. AQUARIUM : FISH ::
  (A) church : canines
  (B) edifice : lawn
  (C) mosque : worshipers
  (D) prayer book : minister
  (E) lobster : boat

____ 73. BALMY : BREEZE ::
  (A) crazy : palm trees
  (B) windy : kite
  (C) cold : sleet
  (D) irritating : coffer
  (E) biased : confusion

____ 74. BEDLAM : CHAOTIC ::
  (A) rivulet : upsetting
  (B) food : quenching
  (C) puzzle : colloquial
  (D) riot : violent
  (E) ultimatum : amusing

____ 75. BESIEGE : FORT ::
  (A) entertain : honor
  (B) plan : trip
  (C) build : buffet
  (D) climb : steppe
  (E) rejoice : mourner

____ 76. BIAS : PREJUDICE ::
  (A) helmet : armor
  (B) altitude : mountain
  (C) violin : fiddle
  (D) verification : question
  (E) coffer : treasure

____ 77. BOURGEOIS : UNCONVENTIONAL ::
  (A) colloquial : formal
  (B) leafy : fertile
  (C) dedicated : sensible
  (D) worthless : stolen
  (E) meticulous : mature

____ 78. BUFFET : DINING ROOM ::
  (A) sedan : automobile
  (B) canine : cartoons
  (C) bed : closet
  (D) tub : bathroom
  (E) living room : edifice

____ 79. CLEMENCY : MERCY ::
  (A) forgiveness : blame
  (B) obedience : law
  (C) seamstress : yardstick
  (D) essay : theme
  (E) criminal : victim

____ 80. COFFER : SAFEGUARD ::
  (A) calculator : multiply
  (B) merchant : cook
  (C) edifice : tumble
  (D) feather : pluck
  (E) canine : sneeze

____ 81. COLLOQUIAL : SLANG ::
  (A) modern : castle
  (B) vulnerable : strength
  (C) defunct : lesson
  (D) balmy : boat
  (E) creative : artist

____ 82. CONCESSION : PRIVILEGE ::
  (A) loser : game
  (B) devastation : rebuilding
  (C) antique : chair
  (D) fork : utensil
  (E) latitude : longitude

Name _____ Date _____ Class _____

___ 83. DEVASTATION : HURRICANE ::
(A) design : plan
(B) decision : discussion
(C) vegetation : rose
(D) rivulet : oasis
(E) healing : medicine

___ 84. DISSENT : ARGUMENT ::
(A) history : era
(B) praise : pride
(C) tax : apple
(D) article : account
(E) switch : power

___ 85. EDIFICE : BUILD ::
(A) occupation : hire
(B) satire : praise
(C) film : direct
(D) ultimatum : require
(E) office : report

___ 86. EMANCIPATE : LIBERATOR ::
(A) need : thief
(B) placate : pacifist
(C) betray : knight
(D) eradicate : building
(E) plant : receptionist

___ 87. ERRATIC : REGULAR ::
(A) bourgeois : middle class
(B) broken : cracked
(C) hesitant : certain
(D) comfortable : mobile
(E) defunct : civilized

___ 88. FROG : LEAP ::
(A) captive : emancipate
(B) prelude : conclude
(C) swimmer : lapse
(D) turtle : speed
(E) canine : howl

___ 89. HIEROGLYPHICS : EGYPT ::
(A) handle : shovel
(B) oasis : desert
(C) mosque : design
(D) archaeologist : scientist
(E) alphabet : affidavit

___ 90. LATITUDE : RESTRICTION ::
(A) nap : sleep
(B) introduction : conclusion
(C) teacher : lecture
(D) arrangement : ultimatum
(E) clemency : pardon

___ 91. MANNERISM : ACTOR ::
(A) coffer : waiter
(B) dance : magician
(C) project : canine
(D) thermometer : nurse
(E) affidavit : minister

___ 92. METICULOUS : CAREFUL ::
(A) observant : noticeable
(B) destructive : erratic
(C) fatal : harmful
(D) besieged : anxious
(E) cheap : expensive

___ 93. MODERATION : EXCESS ::
(A) melody : music
(B) kindness : meanness
(C) mice : barn
(D) remark : comment
(E) fine : penalty

___ 94. OBLITERATE : CREATE ::
(A) read : study
(B) purge : devise
(C) demolish : construct
(D) harm : dissent
(E) think : ponder

___ 95. PRONE : FLAT ::
(A) lethal : fatal
(B) hairy : feathered
(C) athletic : fantastic
(D) oval : circular
(E) deceitful : friendless

___ 96. PURGE : RID ::
(A) imprison : decimate
(B) hold : release
(C) notify : inform
(D) bias : improve
(E) grow : harvest

USING NEW WORDS ON TESTS 57

___ **97.** QUANTITATIVE : ECONOMICS ::
   (A) genuine : concession
   (B) flexible : cash
   (C) bourgeois : cause
   (D) frustrating : latitude
   (E) adventurous : trek

___ **98.** RIVULET : RIVER ::
   (A) canoe : rapids
   (B) steppe : mountain
   (C) path : road
   (D) brook : bedlam
   (E) buffet : dresser

___ **99.** STEPPE : RUSSIA ::
   (A) latitude : geography
   (B) mosque : ocean
   (C) coat : closet
   (D) capital : cloud
   (E) highway : freeway

___ **100.** ULTIMATUM : DIPLOMAT ::
   (A) strategy : coach
   (B) buffet : customer
   (C) glue : paper
   (D) gift : present
   (E) canine : kennel

Using New Words on Tests

Test 3 — CONTEXT: The Environment

Making New Words Your Own Lessons 21–30
Connecting New Words and Patterns Lessons 11–15
Reading New Words in Context Lessons 11–15

PART A • Critical Reading

Directions. Read the following passage. Then circle the letter of the correct answer to each of the twenty items that follow it. The numbers of the items are the same as the numbers of the boldface vocabulary words in the passage. *(1 point each)*

Topic: Global Warming

On an especially hot August day, Josh and Darla Brandt were playing chess at the kitchen table. Darla blocked one of Josh's chessmen, and he groaned with displeasure. His sister often beat him at chess, but today Josh was playing more poorly than usual. He was beginning to get anxious and flustered. He couldn't focus on making his next move.

"Don't get so frustrated," Darla advised him. "Just keep calm. The key to playing chess is to keep your cool—maintain an emotional **equilibrium** (1). If you don't stay balanced and calm, you'll just start making careless moves."

Mr. Brandt walked into the kitchen as Darla was talking. "Speaking of **equilibrium**," he said, "on days like this I wonder if the whole environment is out of whack. This is the hottest week I can remember."

"I hope you're not going to start talking about global warming and the greenhouse effect again, Dad," Darla groaned. "I just don't buy that **scenario** (2); it sounds like the outline for the script of a bad science fiction movie. How can scientists predict step by step what's going to happen to the environment?"

"Darla, sometimes you're just too **naive** (3) for words," Josh said. "You have about as much insight into environmental problems as a gerbil."

"There's no need to be insulting, Josh," Mr. Brandt said. "Global warming isn't a **theoretical** (4) problem; there's plenty of evidence that it actually is taking place. Many factual studies—real **documentary** (5) evidence—show that the earth is getting hotter, and many scientists believe the trend is a result of heat-causing gases trapped in the atmosphere."

"But some scientists disagree with that conclusion," Darla argued. "The warming may be from volcanic eruptions or from sunspots. We may just be in a natural **transition** (6) from one kind of climate to another. After all, the environment has been changing gradually for millions of years."

"I think scientists who take that approach are just **quibbling** (7)—trying to avoid the point by focusing on details that don't have anything to do with what's really going on," Josh said. "I suppose you think that it's just accidental, or **coincidental** (8), that heat records are being broken again and again.

"Temperatures just **fluctuate** (9) naturally, changing from year to year," Darla explained. "It's no big deal."

"I think you're wrong about that," Mr. Brandt said. "The greenhouse effect is related to the earth's warming; the temperature changes are not **irrelevant** (10), or beside the point. Most scientists are convinced that global warming *is* a big deal, and they blame rising temperatures on the greenhouse effect. Specifically, they blame so-called greenhouse gases—especially water vapor, carbon dioxide, methane, and chlorofluorocarbons. More of these gases are in our atmosphere than ever before. Like glass in a greenhouse, the gases let the sunlight in but don't let the heat out.

"The buildup of gases is heavy enough to be noticed," Mr. Brandt continued, "so we're not talking about tiny amounts. For example, the amount of carbon dioxide in the atmosphere is not up just a little but **substantially** (11)—by more than 20 percent in the last one hundred years."

Josh interrupted, "Isn't the intense heat on Venus caused mostly by the amount of carbon dioxide in its atmosphere?"

"Yes," Mr. Brandt said. "Because of the makeup of Venus's atmosphere, the heat is constant rather than **intermittent** (12). And, of course, the heat is intense; the atmosphere there would make your blood boil."

"I don't think anybody's talking about the earth becoming another Venus—not any time soon anyway," Darla said.

"No," Josh said, "but some of the predictions of what could happen because of global warming are **disconcerting** (13), disturbing, and truly frightening. We can't be **oblivious** (14) to them, like an ostrich with its head in the sand."

"I just don't believe that it will get that bad," Darla said.

"Judge for yourself, Darla," Mr. Brandt said. "Here's a magazine article that gives a summary, a **synopsis** (15), of what could happen as a result of global warming. Some of the possibilities include terrible heat waves and droughts, violent weather, severe crop losses and the resulting rising food prices, water shortages, rising sea levels, and displaced populations. Most responsible scientists say that something needs to be done. To focus on other issues and be **indifferent** (16) to this problem may mean that a hotter, more unpleasant planet will be the **legacy** (17) that you will inherit."

"Well, I've read that such predictions are based on computer models," Darla said, "and they may or may not be right. Computers aren't free from error, you know. They aren't **infallible** (18)."

"They're accurate enough to convince me," Josh said. "I think it would be absurd and senseless—in fact, downright **irrational** (19)—to ignore the evidence. It's right before our eyes."

"OK, let's say you're right," Darla said with a tone in her voice that suggested she was starting to agree with them. "What are we supposed to do about it?"

"Global warming cannot be **rectified** (20), or remedied, overnight. It's a complex problem, and the solutions are equally complex and varied," Mr. Brandt said. "One thing we know, however, is that we need to stop relying on fossil fuels and develop and use more renewable energy sources."

"Well, I guess I could start riding my bike to school," Darla said. Her voice trailed off, and she grew thoughtful as she absentmindedly made another move on the chessboard. Josh saw his chance.

"Checkmate!" he announced, his voice triumphant.

Name _____ Date _____ Class _____

1. In the preceding passage, **equilibrium** means
   (A) carefulness
   (B) complaint
   (C) weakness
   (D) structure
   (E) balance

2. In the preceding passage, **scenario** means
   (A) scenery for a theatrical event
   (B) documents that are for sale
   (C) outline of proposed events
   (D) scientific experiment
   (E) evidence of global warming

3. In the preceding passage, **naive** means
   (A) environmentally sound
   (B) lacking insight
   (C) gerbil-shaped
   (D) self-destructive
   (E) problem causing

4. In the preceding passage, **theoretical** means
   (A) thinking
   (B) insulting
   (C) natural
   (D) unproven
   (E) actual

5. In the preceding passage, **documentary** means
   (A) based on supporting references
   (B) subject to controversy and debate
   (C) pertaining to the health of the environment
   (D) not considered factual
   (E) available to the public

6. In the preceding passage, **transition** means
   (A) nature
   (B) climate
   (C) theory
   (D) argument
   (E) change

7. In the preceding passage, **quibbling** means
   (A) causing an accident
   (B) joining in the discussion
   (C) avoiding the point
   (D) explaining a theory
   (E) showing interest

8. In the preceding passage, **coincidental** means
   (A) accidental
   (B) recorded
   (C) actual
   (D) controversial
   (E) warmest

9. In the preceding passage, **fluctuate** means
   (A) change once
   (B) never change
   (C) change continually
   (D) rise year after year
   (E) fall at a regular rate

10. In the preceding passage, **irrelevant** means
    (A) applicable
    (B) unrelated
    (C) sensible
    (D) specific
    (E) convincing

11. In the preceding passage, **substantially** means
    (A) one in a hundred
    (B) atmospherically
    (C) not considerably
    (D) unimportantly
    (E) significantly

12. In the preceding passage, **intermittent** means
    (A) intense
    (B) constant
    (C) occasional
    (D) boiling
    (E) interesting

13. In the preceding passage, **disconcerting** means
    (A) disturbing
    (B) intense
    (C) pleasant
    (D) necessary
    (E) accidental

14. In the preceding passage, **oblivious** means
    (A) opposed
    (B) contented
    (C) evident
    (D) unaware
    (E) fearful

USING NEW WORDS ON TESTS 61

15. In the preceding passage, **synopsis** means
    (A) summary
    (B) article
    (C) proposal
    (D) magazine
    (E) denial

16. In the preceding passage, **indifferent** means
    (A) specific
    (B) unconcerned
    (C) involved
    (D) unessential
    (E) agitated

17. In the preceding passage, **legacy** means
    (A) legality
    (B) inheritance
    (C) magazine
    (D) opinion
    (E) unpleasantness

18. In the preceding passage, **infallible** means
    (A) based on computer models
    (B) newspaper stories
    (C) understandable predictions
    (D) lack of understanding
    (E) free from error

19. In the preceding passage, **irrational** means
    (A) sensible
    (B) accurate
    (C) illogical
    (D) unnecessary
    (E) illegal

20. In the preceding passage, **rectified** means
    (A) activated
    (B) remedied
    (C) affected
    (D) varied
    (E) ignored

PART B • Sentence Completion

Directions. For each of the following items, circle the letter of the choice that best completes the meaning of the sentence or sentences. *(1 point each)*

21. There's no point in dwelling on the fact that humanity has _____ the job of caring for our planet. It's still not too late to make amends for our poor performance.
    (A) simulated
    (B) botched
    (C) rectified
    (D) edified
    (E) merged

22. New policies are needed to ensure that global warming does not become life-threatening, like a _____ disease in our environment.
    (A) translucent
    (B) incendiary
    (C) pallid
    (D) subsidiary
    (E) malignant

23. The studies of Swedish chemist Svante Arrhenius in 1896 relate to the buildup of carbon dioxide in the atmosphere. Therefore, these studies are _____ to global warming.
    (A) pertinent
    (B) caustic
    (C) demure
    (D) incendiary
    (E) theoretical

24. Arrhenius carefully _____ over the idea that the use of coal in Europe could increase carbon dioxide in the atmosphere and _____ in global warming.
    (A) gloated . . . end
    (B) laughed . . . rectify
    (C) convened . . . freeze
    (D) thought . . . protrude
    (E) mulled . . . result

25. Like the _____ of a family, Arrhenius was concerned about future generations and their well-being.
    (A) patent
    (B) arbiter
    (C) crony
    (D) patriarch
    (E) episode

26. A 1957 study by Scripps Institution of Oceanography found that the amount of carbon dioxide released by industries was not _____ but quite significant.
    (A) oblivious
    (B) resonant
    (C) negligible
    (D) pertinent
    (E) caustic

27. The force, or _____, of the worldwide concern about global warming began to build during a 1988 Senate hearing.
    (A) reprieve
    (B) momentum
    (C) closure
    (D) indifference
    (E) requiem

28. During the hearing, NASA scientist James Hansen _____ the theory of global warming and captured world _____. His thorough explanation caused many people to become concerned about the greenhouse effect.
    (A) fluctuated . . . rejection
    (B) debased . . . carelessness
    (C) preached . . . jargon
    (D) resonated . . . publicity
    (E) explicated . . . attention

29. The hearing, which for many was their introduction to the problem, could be called a sort of _____ of global warming as a _____ actor on the world environmental stage.
    (A) debut . . . leading
    (B) imposition . . . failing
    (C) episode . . . silent
    (D) decline . . . sardonic
    (E) sign . . . melancholy

30. Hansen's warnings about global warming did not seem _____ with reality because that same year there was severe drought and heat.
    (A) redundant
    (B) intermittent
    (C) inconsistent
    (D) translucent
    (E) pertinent

31. When Hansen said he was 99 percent ____ that the greenhouse effect had started, the explosion of controversy he set off made it seem as if a bomb had been ____ in the environmental movement.
    (A) unsure . . . ejected
    (B) livid . . . made
    (C) sporadic . . . defused
    (D) certain . . . detonated
    (E) pertinent . . . dropped

32. A number of environmental conferences have been ____ so that scientists can meet in groups to study the ____ of global warming.
    (A) indicted . . . reaction
    (B) rejected . . . stimulant
    (C) detonated . . . destruction
    (D) convened . . . problem
    (E) held . . . rendezvous

33. Scientists who support global warming theory meet one another at these conferences; some who don't support it also ____ there.
    (A) wheedle
    (B) jostle
    (C) rendezvous
    (D) abdicate
    (E) stipulate

34. Many people think that companies should not be given ____ from submitting to environmental laws, because such delays just make matters worse.
    (A) transitions
    (B) legacies
    (C) reprieves
    (D) scenarios
    (E) rebukes

35. We cannot afford to listen to ____ from public officials. Instead, we need sincere talk that produces real action.
    (A) clangor
    (B) parody
    (C) explication
    (D) cant
    (E) closure

36. This is not the time for the public to ____ the efforts of environmentalists to combat the greenhouse effect. Action is needed, not ridicule.
    (A) debut
    (B) indict
    (C) stipulate
    (D) eject
    (E) parody

37. Awareness on the part of public officials can be the ____, or incentive, that causes them to pass the laws necessary to protect the environment.
    (A) stimulant
    (B) sequel
    (C) momentum
    (D) synthesis
    (E) finish

38. Some people still need to be ____ about the dangers of destroying tropical forests, yet many have already been enlightened about how such destruction ____ to global warming.
    (A) detonated . . . leads
    (B) stipulated . . . turns
    (C) edified . . . contributes
    (D) asked . . . fluctuates
    (E) enjoined . . . passes

39. Education of the public is the first step in the efforts to slow global warming. A ____ would, hopefully, be the implementation of corrective measures by the public.
    (A) synthesis
    (B) scenario
    (C) synopsis
    (D) sequel
    (E) lexicon

40. The TV crew's ____ this week includes five states in the Northeast. Their route next week covers seven states in the Midwest.
    (A) stratagem
    (B) synthesis
    (C) imposition
    (D) episode
    (E) itinerary

41. Scientists use computer models of the atmosphere to _____ possible future climatic conditions. These models show how different variables affect the earth's climate.
    (A) rectify
    (B) reprieve
    (C) simulate
    (D) convene
    (E) create

42. Some companies may consider such laws an _____, but experts say it will not be difficult for the companies to _____.
    (A) itinerary . . . resist
    (B) intuition . . . reply
    (C) episode . . . fight
    (D) imposition . . . cooperate
    (E) invitation . . . botch

43. The world's producers of chlorofluorocarbons, chemicals that contribute to the destruction of the ozone layer, have agreed to phase out most of their production. Because the agreement is legally binding, producers could be _____ to comply; however, the countries that agreed to phase out these chemicals have already done so.
    (A) abdicated
    (B) rankled
    (C) enjoined
    (D) reprieved
    (E) wheedled

44. Call it a hunch, but my _____ told me that the world's major countries would support _____ to reduce carbon emissions.
    (A) stimulant . . . actions
    (B) intuition . . . efforts
    (C) lexicon . . . words
    (D) hope . . . cant
    (E) patriarch . . . nothing

45. Like military leaders planning _____, policymakers must devise schemes to make the world less reliant on fossil fuels.
    (A) momentum
    (B) synthesis
    (C) rendezvous
    (D) stratagems
    (E) synopsis

46. Global warming could result in the _____ of various businesses as families leave their jobs and _____ to better climates.
    (A) equilibrium . . . vote
    (B) momentum . . . join
    (C) closure . . . relocate
    (D) potency . . . leave
    (E) opening . . . condole

47. Mrs. Potts, who turned ninety last week, was in a _____ mood as she told about some of the hot summers she recalled from her childhood in Alabama. At times, it was even too hot for her to _____ her pony. She had to give up riding when she couldn't straddle a horse.
    (A) theoretical . . . bestride
    (B) redundant . . . jostle
    (C) sordid . . . fluctuate
    (D) reminiscent . . . bestride
    (E) demure . . . edify

48. The council's second study on the local effects of global warming was so much like its first study that people felt it was _____.
    (A) pertinent
    (B) redundant
    (C) odious
    (D) inconsistent
    (E) infallible

49. The _____ of the alarm bell for global warming has become even louder. Scientists say global warming will increase at a faster _____ now.
    (A) patent . . . time
    (B) scenario . . . rate
    (C) sound . . . sequel
    (D) jargon . . . speed
    (E) clangor . . . pace

50. Although there was some _____ about these models in the past, scientists are no longer subject to disapproval and _____ for accepting the predictions of the models. Most scientists now accept the use of climatic models as reasonable and necessary.
    (A) misunderstanding . . . indictment
    (B) controversy . . . rebuke
    (C) parody . . . rejection
    (D) fluctuation . . . questioning
    (E) legacy . . . rebuke

USING NEW WORDS ON TESTS 65

Name _____ Date _____ Class _____

51. Results vary in the predictions of climatic models because nothing _____, or specifies, which equations scientists must use.
(A) mortifies
(B) states
(C) detonates
(D) convenes
(E) stipulates

52. Industries are discovering that they cannot _____ when it comes to environmental issues. It's impossible to waver in dealing with such recognizable problems as global warming.
(A) fluctuate
(B) explicate
(C) mull
(D) rebuke
(E) eject

53. The speaker warned that anyone who engaged in violent protests would be forcibly _____ from the conference.
(A) rebuked
(B) debased
(C) thronged
(D) ejected
(E) jostled

54. By pleading with and flattering our environmentally conscious parents, my sister and I _____ them into buying a more fuel-efficient car.
(A) rebuked
(B) jostled
(C) wheedled
(D) debased
(E) quibbled

55. In a moment of carelessness, I _____ threw away my report on global warming. Fortunately, I had given a copy to the school _____ just in case I needed to do additional research.
(A) infallibly . . . principal
(B) inadvertently . . . library
(C) decrepitly . . . coach
(D) substantially . . . staff
(E) purposely . . . patriarch

56. The speaker favors _____ programs for reforestation as well as required forest-preservation rules.
(A) obligatory
(B) melancholy
(C) indifferent
(D) sporadic
(E) immaculate

57. Sometimes I feel _____ that people have poisoned the earth's atmosphere, but anger and outrage do not help.
(A) naive
(B) melancholy
(C) livid
(D) vehement
(E) odious

58. To understand the greenhouse effect, you must realize that the glass in a greenhouse is transparent, not merely _____.
(A) translucent
(B) livid
(C) effervescent
(D) malignant
(E) redundant

59. The newspaper editorial said that a certain king should _____ his throne because he refuses to use his power and authority to support _____ efforts to slow global warming.
(A) jostle . . . shaky
(B) eject . . . unpopular
(C) convene . . . publicized
(D) abdicate . . . international
(E) condole . . . unnecessary

60. Some people in the crowd at Tuesday's environmental rally _____ one another as they pushed forward to get a _____ view of the famous speaker.
(A) stipulated . . . farther
(B) jostled . . . better
(C) rebuked . . . higher
(D) helped . . . demure
(E) debased . . . hopeful

61. Three _____ protesters succeeded in stirring up trouble for a brief time during the speech.
    (A) negligible
    (B) impartial
    (C) incendiary
    (D) demure
    (E) sporadic

62. A major polluter promised to replace its old, _____, out-of-date machinery with new equipment that uses geothermal energy.
    (A) decrepit
    (B) incendiary
    (C) irksome
    (D) redundant
    (E) sordid

63. Perhaps you have read about _____ for inventions that will help us _____ renewable energy sources such as hydrogen.
    (A) documentaries . . . stop
    (B) parodies . . . enjoy
    (C) sequels . . . ignore
    (D) ideas . . . mortify
    (E) patents . . . use

64. One company's _____ of its stated obligation to fund research for renewable energy sources _____ the public, who felt that an important promise had been broken.
    (A) parody . . . disgusted
    (B) rebuke . . . pleased
    (C) statement . . . botched
    (D) breach . . . angered
    (E) episode . . . amused

65. Because he did not take sides in the debate about global warming, the scientist was considered to be _____.
    (A) pallid
    (B) irrational
    (C) impartial
    (D) infallible
    (E) translucent

66. Because the _____ of the scientists' arguments to ban certain gases was strong, even the most doubting members of the audience were _____.
    (A) jargon . . . bored
    (B) legacy . . . deaf
    (C) potency . . . convinced
    (D) equilibrium . . . angry
    (E) momentum . . . stopped

67. Although most supporters of the environmental movement act from noble motives, some act from less than noble, even _____, motives.
    (A) immaculate
    (B) infallible
    (C) theoretical
    (D) sordid
    (E) naive

68. Governmental agencies may join to more effectively _____ with environmental issues. United, they can strive to better monitor global warming problems.
    (A) daunt
    (B) bestride
    (C) quibble
    (D) condole
    (E) contend

69. One president was _____ when she found out that her company was guilty of putting so many dangerous chemicals into the _____. She vowed to translate her deep embarrassment into actions to help clean up the air.
    (A) effervescent . . . water fountain
    (B) demure . . . stores
    (C) incendiary . . . laboratory
    (D) mortified . . . atmosphere
    (E) oblivious . . . company

70. A new TV series focuses on various aspects of the environment. Tuesday night's _____ will be about global warming and the greenhouse effect.
    (A) casement
    (B) legacy
    (C) synthesis
    (D) episode
    (E) transition

USING NEW WORDS ON TESTS

Name _____ Date _____ Class _____

PART C • Analogies

Directions. For each of the following items, choose the lettered pair of words that expresses a relationship that is most similar to the relationship between the pair of capitalized words. Write the letter of your answer on the line provided before the number of the item. *(1 point each)*

_____ **71.** ARBITER : DECIDE ::
    (A) casement : squeak
    (B) advisor : advance
    (C) architect : design
    (D) transition : change
    (E) crop : harvest

_____ **72.** CASEMENT : WINDOW ::
    (A) frostbite : winter
    (B) cafeteria : restaurant
    (C) limousine : chauffeur
    (D) uniform : officer
    (E) shelter : attic

_____ **73.** CAUSTIC : SARCASM ::
    (A) frightening : comedy
    (B) inconsistent : argument
    (C) livid : sunshine
    (D) baked : recipe
    (E) hollow : cavity

_____ **74.** CONDOLE : SYMPATHIZER ::
    (A) skip : sidewalk
    (B) celebrate : winner
    (C) whistle : singer
    (D) slice : scissors
    (E) destroy : rescuer

_____ **75.** CONVINCED : CERTAIN ::
    (A) precise : careless
    (B) pertinent : unrelated
    (C) translucent : empty
    (D) immaculate : pure
    (E) simple : original

_____ **76.** CRONY : BUDDY ::
    (A) motive : crime
    (B) scenario : scenery
    (C) duty : obligation
    (D) patriarch : generation
    (E) acquaintance : introduction

_____ **77.** DEBASE : ELEVATE ::
    (A) develop : perform
    (B) plant : grow
    (C) nibble : devour
    (D) criticize : praise
    (E) jump : leap

_____ **78.** DEMURE : FLASHY ::
    (A) coincidental : unplanned
    (B) plain : fancy
    (C) obligatory : required
    (D) delicate : frail
    (E) bright : brilliant

_____ **79.** EARNEST : SINCERE ::
    (A) romantic : sullen
    (B) intense : calm
    (C) vehement : passionate
    (D) oblivious : aware
    (E) naive : awkward

_____ **80.** EFFERVESCENT : LISTLESS ::
    (A) brilliant : dull
    (B) infallible : accurate
    (C) sordid : silly
    (D) true : factual
    (E) feverish : restless

_____ **81.** GENTLE : BREEZE ::
    (A) temporary : closure
    (B) resonant : cello
    (C) redundant : memory
    (D) crunchy : milk
    (E) purple : lemon

_____ **82.** GLOAT : ENJOY ::
    (A) acknowledge : ignore
    (B) glare : look
    (C) rebuke : praise
    (D) mull : worry
    (E) travel : ride

Name _____ Date _____ Class _____

____ 83. INDICT : GRAND JURY ::
(A) rule : monarch
(B) vote : laws
(C) wheedle : gift
(D) argue : decision
(E) edify : criminal

____ 84. IRKSOME : PEST ::
(A) geographic : breakfast
(B) amusing : clown
(C) endless : adventure
(D) dry : waves
(E) hungry : meal

____ 85. JOURNALISTS : REPORTERS ::
(A) class : teachers
(B) episodes : actors
(C) physician : patients
(D) patents : inventions
(E) clientele : customers

____ 86. LEXICON : REFERENCE BOOK ::
(A) understanding : explanation
(B) clangor : bell
(C) chapter : book
(D) Judaism : religion
(E) legacy : ancestor

____ 87. LOCATE : FIND ::
(A) explicate : think
(B) jostle : crowd
(C) flatter : nag
(D) offend : lose
(E) carp : complain

____ 88. MELANCHOLY : GLOOM ::
(A) merchant : buyer
(B) tradition : custom
(C) quibbling : resentment
(D) stratagem : enemy
(E) mood : caution

____ 89. PALLID : PALE ::
(A) negligible : noticeable
(B) quiet : hushed
(C) pure : polluted
(D) irrational : emotional
(E) vicious : virtuous

____ 90. PLATEAU : ELEVATED ::
(A) jargon : unintelligible
(B) intuition : learned
(C) advent : excited
(D) treat : ordinary
(E) fabric : wooden

____ 91. PROTRUDE : JUT OUT ::
(A) doze : sleepwalk
(B) allow : forbid
(C) reshape : carve
(D) remember : recall
(E) listen : understand

____ 92. RANKLE : SOOTHE ::
(A) burst : swell
(B) frighten : capture
(C) broil : boil
(D) uplift : inspire
(E) enjoy : dislike

____ 93. REALISTIC : FANTASTIC ::
(A) impartial : important
(B) smelly : fishy
(C) odious : appealing
(D) irrelevant : unimportant
(E) adorable : cute

____ 94. REQUIEM : HONOR ::
(A) novel : entertain
(B) momentum : stop
(C) rendezvous : miss
(D) cemetery : design
(E) solo : sleep

____ 95. SARDONIC : SARCASTIC ::
(A) rare : worthless
(B) tasty : sour
(C) famous : wealthy
(D) fantastic : ordinary
(E) cheerful : glad

____ 96. SPORADIC : OCCASIONAL ::
(A) preferred : selective
(B) considerate : thoughtful
(C) equal : lopsided
(D) musical : dramatic
(E) strict : cautious

USING NEW WORDS ON TESTS

____ 97. SUBSIDIARY : SECONDARY ::
   (A) busy : bored
   (B) loud : unpleasant
   (C) swollen : shrunken
   (D) strange : odd
   (E) victorious : defeated

____ 98. SYNTHESIS : CHEMIST ::
   (A) parting : separation
   (B) statue : artist
   (C) camera : lens
   (D) thirst : liquid
   (E) branch : limb

____ 99. THRONG : CROWD ::
   (A) tension : relaxation
   (B) love : emotion
   (C) physician : patient
   (D) melody : tune
   (E) ocean : water

____ 100. TRAGEDY : SAD ::
   (A) appetizer : tasty
   (B) itinerary : confusing
   (C) farce : funny
   (D) audience : absent
   (E) requiem : cheerful

Notes

Notes

Notes

Notes

Notes

Notes